Captivity To Eternity
DANIEL
God's Faithful Servant

COMMENTARY AND BIBLE STUDY
ON THE BOOK OF DANIEL

Ronald A. Clower

WESTBOW
PRESS®
A DIVISION OF THOMAS NELSON
& ZONDERVAN

Scripture taken from the King James Version of the Bible.

Scripture taken from the Holy Bible, NEW INTERNATIONAL VERSION®. Copyright © 1973, 1978, 1984 by Biblica, Inc. All rights reserved worldwide. Used by permission. NEW INTERNATIONAL VERSION® and NIV® are registered trademarks of Biblica, Inc. Use of either trademark for the offering of goods or services requires the prior written consent of Biblica US, Inc.

Literary Editor: Cheryl A. Clower
Contributing Editor: Brian P. Beatty
Artwork and Illustrations: Ronald A. Clower
Graphics Editor: Justin A. Clower

WestBow Press books may be ordered through booksellers or by contacting:

WestBow Press
A Division of Thomas Nelson & Zondervan
1663 Liberty Drive
Bloomington, IN 47403
www.westbowpress.com
1 (866) 928-1240

ISBN: 978-1-4908-9110-1 (sc)
ISBN: 978-1-4908-9109-5 (e)

Library of Congress Control Number: 2015911038

Print information available on the last page.

WestBow Press rev. date: 08/03/2015

Dedication

This book is joyfully dedicated to every Christian believer who faithfully

pick up their Bibles daily to read and dwell on God's Word and

seek His divine purpose and guidance for their lives.

Contents

Preface

Captivity to Eternity, Daniel, God's Faithful Servant, herein referred to as "Daniel," has evolved over several seasons of intense study and research into a concise verse-by-verse study of the Book of Daniel. This is my second book installment in my personal journey to understanding God's prophesies and eternal plan for mankind, including His covenant people – the nation of Israel. "Daniel" is a direct commission from God, the Holy Spirit given to me while reading through this Old Testament book during my annual cover-to-cover Bible reading in 2013.

God is omniscient and omnipotent. His plan for mankind, including His covenant people, Israel is sovereign and cannot be thwarted. Daniel was the man God chose to chronicle His eternal plan, and He accomplished this through a series of prophetic dreams and visions given to the prophet over the span of his life while in captivity. From his early years as a Hebrew teen exiled from his homeland to his adult years as a trusted adviser to the kings of Babylon, and later as a loyal senior administrator to Persia, God used Daniel as His faithful servant to convert the hearts and minds of many Gentile rulers of the times. Daniel's faith influenced and shaped the affairs of these world empires according to God's plan, and his prophetic visions further defined God's plan beyond Daniel's life and into the distant future. His prophecies were endorsed centuries later by our Lord Jesus Christ (Matthew 24:15) and developed further by the Apostle John in the New Testament Book of Revelation.

My goal for this book, as with my former book, *Jesus Christ, The Centerpiece of God's Universe,* herein referred to as "Centerpiece," was to make the study of the Book of Daniel comprehensive but not complex, thorough yet easy to follow. The use of Bible commentary, related subject lessons, personal experiences, and illustrations combine to add redundancy and visual interest to the study. "Daniel" was written to appeal to all ages, from high school youth to adult seniors. Throughout the chapters reference is made to supporting verses located elsewhere in the Scriptures. Some of these passages are quoted in their entirety, while others are left simply in parentheses. Those passages are left unquoted for the purpose of encouraging the reader to dive deeper into the Scriptures. This was why I chose not to include the complete Daniel Bible text in this book (Scripture segments are taken from the NIV, unless otherwise noted). Therefore, it becomes a requirement that the reader always have his or her own personal Bible, whichever version they prefer, to follow along while reading and studying "Daniel." The unquoted passages can also be used, in a classroom setting, to facilitate oral class reading and participation. At the end of each chapter are "Review Questions" meant to highlight and emphasize key elements in order to build upon the reader's knowledge of the message. The "Up For Discussion" sections are optional, and can be used for personal reflection or to facilitate additional classroom discussion on a deeper level. This may include relating the subject matter to current events or encouraging class members to share some of their own personal experiences.

Since the publication of "Centerpiece," my first book and commentary on the Book of Revelation in early 2011, I have had the honor and privilege of traveling throughout my home state, Georgia, promoting it while meeting new Christian believers excited about studying God's Word. I have been invited to speak at a number of churches and to participate in their local Bible study classes. I was also given the honor to present my personal testimony to the congregation at our 2012 year-end Jubilee Celebration Service. In the years that followed, I participated as one of thirty daily bloggers in support of our church's three-year commitment to read through the Bible. I currently serve as a co-facilitator in my adult Sunday school class at our home church, Providence United Methodist, and usually facilitate an in-depth study of the Book of Revelation once a year. Nevertheless, I believe my biggest call and heartfelt commitment is to my on-line ministry and website: CenterpieceMinistries.com. It is on-line and in connection with social media, that I reach out to the world, not only to promote my books, but more importantly, to promote the reading and understanding of God's Word. The website changes monthly with new and insightful Bible commentary and guest insight. I also post my one-year Bible reading calendars, in various formats, and every color illustration from my books. These teaching aids are available on-line for anyone to copy and use in their personal or group Bible study at no charge (copyrights apply). Equally important, I maintain an on-going "Prayer List," because I know that my on-line audience is made up of strong people of faith and mighty prayer warriors who wish to make a difference in the lives of their Christian brethren.

I have grown closer to the Lord with every exercise, but nothing compares to the lesson I learned while working one weekend alongside the Reverend Dan McFarland on an Emmaus Walk. Throughout the weekend I was literally amazed at his knowledge of the Scriptures and how he could quote, by verse, a passage from the Bible that related to whatever it was we were discussing at the time. I asked how he had memorized the Scriptures so well. His reply was simply, "I read the Bible through every year, and I have been doing that for over thirty years." He then gave me a copy of his Bible Reading Calendar. Ever since that day in 2004, I can count on one hand, how many days I have missed reading God's Word. I have since completed ten years of reading the Holy Scriptures, cover to cover. I thank Reverend McFarland for his gift and inspiration, and there is nothing greater I could recommend to anyone then to spend time everyday reading and dwelling on God's Word. I have included a copy of our one-year Bible Reading Calendar at the end of chapter 9 of "Daniel" to encourage you to start your own tradition of reading God's Word daily. I promise you God will honor that commitment in your life. You will come to realize that the Holy Scriptures and the prophecies contained therein, from the first chapters of Genesis to Daniel, and through the last verses of the Revelation, all point to our Messiah and Lord Jesus Christ.

Amen. Come, Lord Jesus.

Introduction

The Book of Daniel is one of the most exciting books in the Bible; and it is, of course, a book on prophecy. One fourth of the books in the Bible are of prophetic nature. Prophecy in Scripture can be divided into fulfilled prophecy and unfulfilled prophecy; in Daniel we will find a great deal of both.

There are many subjects or topics of prophecy found throughout God's Word including those on the nation of Israel, the Gentile nations, the Tribulation Period, the end-time Antichrist, the end of the age, Christ's earthly kingdom, and eternity. There are even prophecies concerning the church, although it is never mentioned in the Old Testament. Furthermore, I believe the finest definition of prophecy in the Scriptures is found in the writings of the Apostle John while imprisoned on the island of Patmos: "For the testimony of Jesus is the spirit of prophecy" (Revelation 19:10). You see all prophecy receives its value and meaning from its relation to Christ. From the first prophetic utterance of God in the Book of Genesis to the last prediction of the Revelation, the heart of prophecy has been directed to the person of Jesus Christ.

Date and Author of Daniel

The Book of Daniel has been a subject of controversy between conservative and liberal scholars for years, arguing over the dating of the writing of the book and its authorship. Some view that long-range predictive prophecy is impossible; and therefore, the book is a forgery written during the Maccabean Period after their fulfillment had taken place. Subsequently, they place its writing around 170 B.C., almost four hundred years after Daniel lived.

The book itself however, mentions Daniel as its author in several passages including 7:15, 8:1, 9:2, and 10:2. The fact that our Lord Jesus Christ agreed is clear from His reference to "the abomination that causes desolation, spoken of through the prophet Daniel" found in His Olivet Discourse (Matthew 24:15). It is interesting to note that our Lord called the Pharisees "hypocrites," but He called Daniel "the prophet." I personally believe that the endorsement of our Lord and Savior is satisfactory enough for all Christians; for that reason I agree with the traditional dating of Daniel written in the sixth century B.C. In addition, the discovery of the Book of Daniel amongst the Dead Sea Scrolls provides even great evidences of their ancient origin and divinely inspired authorship as prophetic Scripture.

We know more about Daniel the man than we do of any other prophet. He gives us a personal account of his life from the time he was carried captive to Babylon in the third year of the reign of Jehoiakim (around 605 B.C.) until the third year of King Cyrus (around 536 B.C.). Daniel's life and ministry thus spans the entire seventy years of Israel's exile. At the beginning of the book, Daniel is a young boy, most likely in his mid-teens. At the end he is an old man of around ninety years. In chapter 10 verse 11 we see God's own appraisal of the man Daniel: "Daniel, you who are highly esteemed."

As we study Daniel we will see that his life was characterized in three ways:

1) Daniel was a man of purpose. Daniel and his friends obeyed God by deciding to follow the Law of Moses and to speak God's Word.
2) Daniel was a man of prayer. There are several incidents recorded in this book about Daniel's prayer life. Remembering the Bible stories from our youth, we will recall that it was prayer that got Daniel thrown into the lions' den.
3) Daniel was a man of prophecy. The Book of Daniel divides itself equally: the first half is history, and the last half is prophecy, some of which is already fulfilled. Daniel gives us a framework of prophecy on which all other prophecy is founded.

The Theme of Daniel

The primary theme or subject for the Book of Daniel is God's sovereignty – God reigns supreme. King Nebuchadnezzar learned this lesson the hard way and in chapter 5 verse 21 we are told "he acknowledged that the Most High God is sovereign over the kingdom of men …." But even earlier, in chapter 2 verse 44, we find the following key verse: "In the time of those kings, the God of heaven will set up a kingdom that will never be destroyed, nor will it be left to another people. It will crush all those kingdoms and bring them to an end, but it will itself endure forever." This is the book of the universal sovereignty of God – He is the ultimate and final authority. In Daniel, prophecy is interwoven with history to show that God is in complete and absolute control of everything throughout all the ages.

Additionally, Daniel brings together "the times of the Gentiles" (Luke 21:24) and the time of the end of "Jacob's trouble" (Jeremiah 30:7) for the nation of Israel during the Great Tribulation Period. This coming time of distress concludes with Christ's return and setting up His Millennial Kingdom on earth. The Book of Daniel answers the question, "Who will rule the world?"

Finally, the Book of Daniel is the key to understanding other Scriptures. Our Lord, in His Olivet Discourse, quoted only from the Book of Daniel (Matthew 24:15). In addition, the Book of Revelation would be largely a mystery or a puzzle without the Book of Daniel. Even the Apostle Paul's revelation concerning the "man of lawlessness" (2 Thessalonians 2:3) needs Daniel's account for meaning and clarification.

Chapter 1

Israel Exiled to Babylon

1:1 – 2: Jehoiakim was placed on the throne of Judah by Pharaoh Neco to replace his brother Jehoahaz, after having him imprisoned and later taken to Egypt where he eventually died. Both Jehoiakim and Jehoahaz were evil sons of Josiah, the godly king during whose reign the book of the law was discovered. Josiah read the book of the law, renewed the covenant, and led the last revival in Judah. Josiah was eventually killed in battle at Megiddo by Neco. Jehoiakim's name was actually Eliakim before being changed to Jehoiakim by Pharaoh Neco (2 Kings 23:34).

Nebuchadnezzar first came against Jerusalem about the year 605 B.C. and took the city in about 602 B.C. His armies confiscated "articles from the temple of God" in fulfillment of Isaiah's prophecy to King Hezekiah first found in 2 Kings 20:12 – 18, and later included in his own writings (Isaiah 39:1 – 6). Jehoiakim served as a "vassal" of King Nebuchadnezzar for three years until such time as he became resentful and emboldened to lead a foolish rebellion against the king. Nevertheless, he was captured, along with the city, shackled, and then "dragged … outside the gates of Jerusalem" where he died and was buried (Jeremiah 22:19). His son Jehoiachin succeeded him as king. At that time, the city was not destroyed, but the first group of exiles was taken to Babylon. Among these were Daniel, his three friends, and thousands of others.

Only some of the articles were taken to Babylon during the first siege; additional treasures and articles of gold from the temple of the Lord were removed later when Jehoiachin surrendered to King Nebuchadnezzar (spring of 597 B.C.) and was also carried into captivity to Babylon. Jerusalem eventually fell to the armies of Nebuchadnezzar during the eleventh year of King Zedekiah in about 586 B.C. It was at this time that the city of Jerusalem, including the temple, was destroyed in flames. The last group of exiles and the remaining articles of bronze, gold, and silver from the temple of the Lord were finally taken to Babylon. We want to keep this in mind, because later in chapter 5 King Belshazzar, probably the grandson of Nebuchadnezzar will bring these gold vessels out for his banquet.

1:3: From every nation he conquered, Nebuchadnezzar always took the best captives for his personal service. Daniel and his three friends were included in this group. The KJV says, "The king spake unto Ashpenaz the master of his eunuchs …." This implies that Daniel and his friends were also made eunuchs. Eunuchs or male servants of a royal palace were often emasculated as a precautionary measure, especially if they served among the wives in a king's harem (2 Kings 9:32). This was in fulfillment of the words of the prophet in Isaiah 39:7.

1:4: The Bible was not written by uneducated men. Just as Moses, educated in all the wisdom of Egypt, wrote the early books of the Bible and the Apostle Paul, a scholarly man of his day, wrote much of the New Testament, so was the case with Daniel. He and his three friends were bright and intelligent young men of their time. They would be taught by others who themselves were well advanced in the knowledge and science of their time.

1:5: Though affluent in nature, the food mentioned here would be basically that of a pagan diet, and would include unclean animals. Daniel was a Jew, and under the Mosaic Law certain meats, fowl, and fish were not to be eaten.

1:6 – 7: The chief official changed their Hebrew names that reflected their devotion to the Lord, to Babylonian names that, instead, reflected their captor's desire to honor their heathen gods:

- Daniel meant "God is my Judge," where the name Belteshazzar meant "worshiper of Baal" or "Bel protect his life," referring to Marduk, their supreme god.
- Hananiah meant "The Lord shows grace," where the name Shadrach meant "command of Aku," referring to the Sumerian moon god.
- Mishael meant "Who is what God is," where the name Meshach meant "Who is what Aku is."
- Azariah meant "The Lord helps," where the name Abednego meant "servant of Nego," referring to the pagan god Nabu.

These four Hebrew young men are singled out and identified for us, and the reason is that they are going to take a stand for God.

1:8: Daniel took a brave stand for God, and he did it in the king's dining hall. The food of Nebuchadnezzar's table was always the very best of the pagan world. However, Daniel and his three friends considered it contaminated because the first portion of it was offered to their pagan idols, as was the wine. In addition unclean animals were used – all illustrating a banquet completely contrary to dietary regulations governed by the Mosaic Law. You see, Daniel would not conform to the world around him; and thus the will of God was the primary purpose of his life. Perhaps Daniel and his three Hebrew friends were Nazirites to whom even wine was forbidden. Regardless, Daniel and his friends were taking a stand under the Law, and they were taking a stand for God.

1:9: You see, Daniel was already "shown favor and sympathy," and that was no accident. God was working on Daniel's behalf just as He did with Joseph, son of Jacob, in Egypt.

1:10: Evidently, the official liked Daniel and his three friends enough to not want to force the diet upon them, but he feared the king. Therefore, he was at a loss as to what to do.

1:11 – 14: Daniel told the guard to "test your servants for ten days." Rather than rebelling, Daniel offered the official an alternative. He assured him that a diet of certain vegetables and water would leave them in as good a condition as the other young men eating the royal food. As we have seen, God had brought favor from this official toward Daniel; thus reluctantly, he resolved to trust Daniel's suggestion and gave him the ten days.

Verse 8 tells us that "Daniel resolved." I like what the KJV says: "Daniel purposed in his heart" – it all began in the heart of Daniel. His convictions came from his heart. Shouldn't that be our experience as well? We are all captives in this world in which we live. Our Lord Jesus said that we are in the world, but not of the world. Daniel purposed in his heart to obey God's law – given to God's people Israel – and this would be his testimony. It should be ours as well.

1:15 – 16: Well, Daniel's diet worked on behalf of all four Hebrews, and that should tell us something. God wanted his people to be different from the other nations around them. The regulations for diet that God gave in His Law were very meaningful for health reasons as well as for ceremonial practices.

Daniel and His Three Friends Excel

1:17: To these four young Hebrew men, who by circumstance found themselves employed in a foreign court, God blessed with "knowledge and understanding of all kinds" just as he did to Joseph while in Egypt. Daniel, as we will see, will eventually become the top ranking official to two great world empires – Babylon and Persia.

Daniel lived during the time of revelation; in other words, a time in which God used dreams and visions to relay his purpose to mankind. Though God may speak to some people in dreams, I believe today that God speaks to us primarily through His written Word. We can't put our Bible under our pillows and expect God to speak to us in our dreams. We have to open it, read it, and study it every day. But here, God was speaking to Daniel because he was writing what would one day become one of the most profound books of prophecy in the Bible.

1:18 – 20: Nebuchadnezzar talked with these four young men and found that they were "ten times" greater in "wisdom and understanding" than all his other officials. Magicians and enchanters mentioned here are most likely priests who claimed to possess occult knowledge and thus were considered valued advisors in the king's court. However, King Nebuchadnezzar considered Daniel and his three friends far better than all others in his kingdom, and accordingly gave them higher positions in his service.

1:21: Combining verse 1 together here with this final verse allows us to somewhat calculate Daniel's life span. Banished to Babylon in his mid-teens, Daniel remained there until the "first year of King Cyrus" of Persia, who conquered Babylon in 539 B.C. As we can see, Daniel's life and career bridged the entire seventy years of captivity. However, we have no record of him returning to Israel or his death.

Review Questions

1) Nebuchadnezzar was King of _____.

2) The name Daniel means _____.

3) Daniel's three Hebrew friends' names were _____.

4) The Babylonian names given to his friends were _____

   _____.

5) What was the purpose of giving them new names? _____

   _____.

6) Why did Daniel and his three friends refuse to eat the royal food? _____

   _____.

7) How did God bless these four young men? _____

   _____.

Up For Discussion

"But Daniel purposed in his heart that he would not defile himself with the portion of
the king's meat, nor with the wine which he drank; therefore he requested of the
prince of the eunuchs that he might not defile himself."
(Daniel 1:8 KJV)

Daniel and his three friends took a courageous stand for God by refusing to eat the royal food provided by King Nebuchadnezzar. They were captives in a foreign land, and under normal circumstances, refusal to comply would have been fatal. However, God was with them and He softened the heart of the chief official and, as a result, he agreed to Daniel's suggestion. As we continue to read the stories of Daniel and his three friends, we will see other examples of how these men refused to conform to the ruling authorities at the risk of their very lives and how they took a stand for God.

Recall the April 1999 tragic shooting at Columbine High School, and how seventeen-year old Cassie Bernall responded "Yes" when asked by her assailant if she believed in God. Have you ever been in a situation where you had to take a stand for God? It may not have been at risk of life, but more likely, at the risk of humiliation by your peers. Maybe you took a stand for God when others remained silence and afterwards was commended for it. Share with the class any related experience you have had.

Chapter 2

The subject of chapter 2 is Nebuchadnezzar's dream of a huge multi-metallic statue and the interpretation Daniel gives regarding the four kingdoms of "the times of the Gentiles."

This is one of the great sections of the Bible as far as prophecy is concerned. The huge multi-metallic statue that we will study in this chapter, along with the four beasts of chapter 7, and the seventy sevens of chapter 9 form the framework of biblical prophecy found in much of the New Testament. Remember that everything the Lord Jesus said in His Olivet Discourse, found in chapters 24 and 25 of Matthew, was based on the Book of Daniel. The disciples asked Jesus, "Tell us, when will this happen, and what will be the sign of your coming and of the end of the age?" Jesus replied, "So when you see standing in the holy place 'the abomination that causes desolation,' spoken of through the prophet Daniel …" (Matthew 24:3, 15).

People everywhere today are asking: "What is this world coming to?" The times of the Gentiles are going to run out (Romans 11:25), and I believe we may come close to seeing that end. However, the church of Jesus Christ will be raptured from this earth before the fullness of the Gentiles is complete. Shortly after the church is removed from the earth, and after seven years of tribulation, Christ will return to earth to establish His earthly kingdom and eternal rule.

Nebuchadnezzar Has a Dream

2:1: Nebuchadnezzar was the oldest son of Nabopolassar, the founder of the Chaldean dynasty of Babylon. He was originally an Assyrian general, but later rebelled and established himself as King of Babylon in 626 B.C. Nebuchadnezzar succeeded his father as king in 605 B.C. and continued in his plans to conquer the surrounding nations, including the Assyrian Empire, Syria, and Egypt. The king even came to marvel about the great empire he had founded. In reality, Babylon was the first great world empire. It was then that God began to speak to Nebuchadnezzar in the form of dreams. The dream in this chapter along with its subsequent interpretation by God's prophet Daniel, make up the most important single prophecy in Scripture concerning the Gentile nations.

2:2 – 3: These men whom the king summoned represented the best seers and occult leaders of Babylon. They were considered wise despite the fact they held many superstitions and concepts of pagan religion. The KJV uses the term "Chaldeans" in place of "astrologers" (NIV). Chaldeans was the term used by many ancient authors to refer to priests and other persons educated in classical Babylonian literature, especially in traditions of astronomy and astrology. It is interesting that some scholars believe the wise men or "Magi from the East" (Matthew 2:1) that came to Jerusalem at the time of Jesus' birth may have been Chaldean astrologers. The term Chaldeans, over time, became synonymous with the term Babylonian.

Babylon, from its very beginning, was considered the birthplace of all false religions. It was in Babylon that Nimrod, grandson of Ham, youngest son of Noah, rebelled against God and initiated a system of pagan religions that emphasized idolatry and sexual immorality. Subsequently, these Chaldeans, or wise men, were advisers in Nebuchadnezzar's court. They were brought before the king to hear an unusual command. The king explained to them that he had a dream which he felt held much significance; however, he did not yet know that the dream was from God.

2:4: It is important to note at this point in the Book of Daniel, from verse 4 here through verse 28 of chapter 7, that the book changes from being written in Hebrew to being written in Aramaic. Though the wise men that made up his court were of various racial backgrounds, Aramaic was the court language and the language they all knew and spoke. It was the language of the Gentiles and the language of the world at that time. The significance is that God, through Daniel, was then speaking to the world, not just to Israel. Israel had gone into Babylonian exile. God had removed the scepter from the line of David, and placed it in the hands of the Gentiles. There it would remain until the day Christ returns to earth to take back the scepter and establish His earthly kingdom; for it is God's ultimate intention for His Son Jesus Christ to reign eternal. These six chapters deal with matters of importance to the Gentile nations of the time and Daniel switched languages because he intended this section to be read by all. Daniel reverted back to Hebrew for the last five chapters (8 – 12) because they dealt with special concerns of God's chosen people – Israel.

2:5 – 6: "Tell me what my dream was and interpret it" was an unusual command from the king. The consequence of failure would be a rather extreme judgment. The king knew the dream, and he sensed its importance. However, he refused to divulge its content to his advisors. Why? I believe the king wanted to get a correct interpretation of it. Nebuchadnezzar was putting fear into these men. On the other hand, Nebuchadnezzar would be generous and charitable to anyone who could tell him the dream and its correct interpretation.

2:7 – 9: The king's servants grasped their dangerous predicament, and once again cautiously tried to get the king to reveal the dream so they could supply an interpretation. But the king meant business and would not allow them to stall. I believe the king was showing his lack of confidence here in his advisors, for they must have failed him before. Nebuchadnezzar felt uneasy with these so-called wise men so he was now subjecting them to a very serious test. His reasoning was quite logical: If they could describe his dream, then their interpretation would most likely be true. If they could not describe his dream, then any interpretation would be questionable.

2:10 – 11: "No one can reveal it to the king except the gods, and they do not live among men." This was the first true statement these advisors had made. In desperation they were pleading for their lives by trying to show how unreasonable the king's demand was. It may even have been an attempt on the king's part to expose the fraudulent schemes of these advisors by issuing such a command. Ironically, even these pagan advisors to the king understood that only a God whose dwelling is not with the "flesh" could describe the dream and its interpretation. This opened the door for Daniel to come onto the scene.

2:12 – 13: The king demonstrated a violent temper, which may be another symptom of the mental illness he suffered from which we will see later. The king ordered all the wise men of Babylon executed, including Daniel and his friends. The king had lost confidence in his royal court of advisors, and therefore, many innocent men would die as a result of his decree.

2:14 – 15: Daniel was perplexed at the rushed injustice of the king's decree, but he was also careful to use "wisdom and tact" in what he said to Arioch. Arioch was the captain of the king's bodyguard, or what we would consider the equivalent to the person in charge of our President's Secret Service.

2:16: Whatever "wisdom" Daniel used in his discourse with Arioch, it worked in granting him an audience with the king. We already learned from chapter 1 verse 19 that the king found favor with Daniel and his friends; thus, for that reason, Daniel asked the king to give him time "so that he might interpret the dream for him." You see, Daniel was a man confident in his faith in God.

2:17 – 18: The glory of God had long departed the temple in Jerusalem, the city laid in ruin, and Israel had gone into exile to Babylon. Despite that, Daniel and his friends knew that God did not dwell in some temple. Daniel called Him "the God of heaven." The KJV further says, "That they would desire mercies." This illustrates the basis of their prayers, and should teach us that all prayer must rest upon His mercy. To pray today in Jesus' name simply means that we come to God, not on our own worth or efforts, but on that of Jesus, looking to Him for mercy. The word "mystery" or "secret" (KJV) refers to secret purposes of God that He reveals only to his prophets and apostles, and are understood by us today only through His Word.

2:19: God revealed the "mystery" to Daniel by giving him the same dream that he gave to Nebuchadnezzar – and only God could do that. God gave Daniel the gift of interpreting the king's dream, just as He did to Joseph with Pharaoh (Genesis 41). God wanted to influence their decisions and accomplish His divine purpose through these kings.

2:20 – 23: This is one of several recorded prayers of Daniel. As I mentioned in our introduction, Daniel was a man of prayer and his heart overflowed with the Spirit of God. God alone had revealed this secret to Daniel, and this was his wonderful prayer of praise and thanksgiving. God had saved his life and the lives of his friends. He also realized from this dream that God had a specific plan for the future of mankind. Daniel was now ready to ask for another audience with the king.

2:24 – 26: Daniel wanted to halt the judgment and execution of the wise men of Babylon, and evidently so did Arioch. Arioch, in turn, rushed Daniel into the presence of the king with good news that his dream would be revealed and interpreted. The king seemed skeptical since none of his other advisors could recount the dream, much less interpret it. Consequently, his question to Daniel sounded rather suspicious. Now let us listen to Daniel's reply.

Daniel Reveals and Interprets the King's Dream

2:27 – 28: Daniel immediately expounded the contrast between the wisdom of this world, that of Babylon, and the wisdom of God. It was the Apostle Paul who wrote: "Has God not made foolish the wisdom of the world? For the foolishness of God is wiser than man's wisdom …" (1 Corinthians 1:20,

25). Daniel was then given the opportunity to introduce this heathen king to the one true living "God in heaven who reveals mysteries." The KJV reads, "In the latter days." This phrase is very important because it is going to be the emphasis in the Book of Daniel. The king's dream refers to the end of "the times of the Gentiles" (Luke 21:24). The conclusion of "the times of the Gentiles" runs concurrently with "the latter days" of the nation of Israel. Both prophecies come to their fulfillment at the close of the Great Tribulation Period. Our Lord Jesus Christ referred to this same time as "the end of the age" (Matthew 13:39). Therefore, Nebuchadnezzar's dream extends from the time of Daniel to the day of Christ's return to earth to establish His eternal kingdom.

We are currently living in the age of grace when God is dealing with mankind through His church. Once the church is removed from earth at the rapture, God will again turn His attention back to the nation of Israel during the Tribulation Period.

2:29 – 30: Nebuchadnezzar was troubled as he lay in bed at night, wondering what the future held now that he was a world ruler.

The dream had to do with the future of Nebuchadnezzar's kingdom and the aftermath of his great world empire. Daniel made it abundantly clear that he deserved no credit, but that God in heaven had revealed the dream so that the king would trust the interpretation. In this pagan land of idolatry, God used the only language that Nebuchadnezzar could understand: the vision of an enormous multi-metallic statue – an idol of worship.

This section shows us the history of the rule of this world by the Gentiles. Because of the corruption and wickedness of the Davidic kings, God removed the scepter of this world from the hands of the line of David, and put it in the hands of the Gentiles. It will remain there until Jesus Christ returns to earth to set up His kingdom and Messianic reign. In other words, from the day of Nebuchadnezzar right on down through today until the Lord Jesus Christ returns to earth constitutes "the times of the Gentiles."

2:31: The statue in the king's dream that Daniel began to describe was "enormous" and "dazzling," and utterly terrifying, yet awe-inspiring as well. Can you imagine the expression on the king's face? His demeanor changed from skepticism to absolute astonishment.

2:32 – 33: As Daniel revealed the dream, I believe Nebuchadnezzar finally began to seriously listen to this young Hebrew and the message from his God. Remember that God was speaking to the king in a language that he could understand. The statue was a tremendous idol with a head of gold, chest and arms of silver, belly and thighs of bronze, legs of iron, and feet of iron and clay composite.

2:34 – 35: We will get this interpretation from Daniel later in verses 44 – 45; however, the reference should be obvious to Christian believers and all students of God's Word. The important thing to note, as the king marveled at this huge statue, was the "rock," cut out "not by human hands," pulverized the image and then grew to "fill the whole earth."

2:36 – 38: Daniel now began to interpret the dream. The four different metals represent Gentile world kingdoms or empires. God made Nebuchadnezzar the one at the top – the head of gold. He made him the first great world ruler with absolute "dominion and power," and there has been none like him since. This was why Daniels called him "the king of kings." More is said about this Babylonian empire throughout the Bible than any other.

2:39: Daniel continued his interpretation. As illustrated by the diminishing value of the metal, the kingdom that followed after Nebuchadnezzar would be inferior to his. The third one, likewise, would be inferior to the second. Recall from chapter 1 that Daniel lived in both the kingdom of Nebuchadnezzar and the second kingdom, that of the Media-Persian Empire. The third kingdom of bronze represents the Greece-Macedonian Empire of Alexander the Great. That brings us to the fourth Gentile kingdom, that of iron – Rome (see end-of-chapter illustration: The Four Gentile Kingdoms).

The diminishing value of the metals from one kingdom to the next suggests a decrease in the absolute power or authority of each king; however, the increasing strength of the metals may suggest an increase of the military strength and technology of each kingdom, resulting in a stronger and more enduring empire. Historically speaking, these four consecutive Gentile kingdoms would dominate the nation of Israel until Christ returns finally to earth to abolish all world empires and establish His eternal kingdom and rule.

2:40 – 43: As we see in these verses, more attention is given to the fourth kingdom than to the other three kingdoms combined. The fourth kingdom is the kingdom of "the latter days." Recall from verse 28, Daniel told Nebuchadnezzar that his vision of the statue concerned the latter days. We are most likely living in the time period today closely leading up to "the latter days."

The legs are of iron, and they represent Rome. The feet of iron and clay composite suggest an unstable or divided form of government in its final form. I believe the clay represents the masses of the different nations of the ten toes; where the iron speaks of the fact that Rome continues to endure. The ten toes of the statue represent ten lesser kings who will turn over their authority in order to rule alongside the final king of the latter days. The ten toes of this chapter and the "ten horns" of Daniel 7:24 are one and the same. The Roman Empire is the last, and it will be revised and in existence in the latter days. All of these other empires were conquered by an enemy from the outside; not so with Rome. Attila the Hun came in and ransacked the city then took his hordes and left. Rome fell apart from within. Today Rome exists in the nations of Europe. The political environment and philosophy of liberal Europe is creating a foundation for the man who is coming someday to put the Roman Empire back together into a final one-world empire. He is known in Scripture as the "man of lawlessness" (2 Thessalonians 2:3), the end-times Antichrist. He is Satan's pawn; and therefore, God will not let him appear until He has called His people and removed His church from the earth at the rapture.

2:44 – 45: These verses represent one of many Old Testament prophecies concerning the coming kingdom of Christ on earth. All the prophets spoke of this kingdom – not one of them missed it. This refers to the time when our Lord and Savior returns to earth as the Righteous Warrior and Judge to "crush" all wickedness and establish His earthly kingdom and Messianic rule. His kingdom will be like that of the head of pure gold, having absolute dominion and authority, only the ruler will be the Rock that is "cut out without human hands" – our Lord Jesus Christ. Jesus is that rock and His kingdom will "endure forever." Jesus, in speaking to the chief priests and the elders, told them: "Have you never read in the Scriptures: The stone the builders rejected has become the capstone" (Matthew 21:42). He went on (in verse 44) to tell them, "He who falls on this stone will be broken to pieces, but he on whom it falls will be crushed." What does that mean to fall on the stone and be broken? It means that when we come to Jesus Christ by faith to be saved, we must "fall" before Him as a sinner, "broken" in spirit with nothing to offer. The Apostle Paul reminds us, "For no one can lay any foundation other than the one already laid, which is Jesus Christ" (1 Corinthians 3:11). Jesus Christ is the Rock of salvation, and He is the Rock of judgment in the latter times.

The reference here is to the second coming of Christ to the earth, which is explained for us in magnificent detail in Revelation 19:11 – 21. We need to trust Jesus Christ as our Lord and Savior. We need to lean on the Rock today; or otherwise, become one of those someday that the Rock falls upon and crushes. Daniel lastly reassured the king that the dream and its interpretation are from God; and thus, they are "trustworthy" and "true."

2:46 – 47: The effect of Daniel's interpretation upon Nebuchadnezzar was obviously profound; but, does the text here mean that the king actually fell down to worship Daniel? The KJV uses the word "worshipped." I believe the king simply did not know how to properly react. Up to this point in his life, he was only familiar with the worship of idols. However, now he intended to worship Daniel's God, the one true living God. This was the king's introduction to the God of heaven, for the king himself called Him "the God of gods and the Lord of kings and a revealer of mysteries." In the book of Daniel, we will watch the evolution in faith of this pagan king as he transitions from heathen darkness into the true light of the knowledge of God.

2:48 – 49: Again, Daniel was rewarded by Nebuchadnezzar; and this time, as stated earlier in chapter 1, he was promoted to the position of highest ranking official in the king's "royal court." Note here that Daniel did not forget his three friends. They likewise received high administrative positions in the government of Babylon. Daniel "remained at the royal court." The KJV uses the phrase, "sat in the gate of the king." To sit at the gate of the king meant to sit as a judge. As we continue our study of Daniel, we will find that he was the man with whom Nebuchadnezzar consulted often. Daniel judged the people; and he was second, only to the king, over of the kingdom of Babylon.

Review Questions

1) Why did Nebuchadnezzar demand that his court advisers reveal to him his dream as well as its interpretation? _____

   _____.

2) Who was it that the wise men claimed could only reveal the dream to the king? _____

   _____.

3) Since these men could not describe the dream, what did the king decree? _____

   _____.

4) The mystery was revealed to Daniel how and by whom? _____

   _____.

5) The dream of an enormous statue made up of metals of diminishing value represents what? ___

   _____.

6) The iron and clay composite structure of the feet of the statue represents what? _____

   _____.

7) Daniel's revelation and interpretation was true, and as a result the king did what? _____

   _____.

Up For Discussion

"And in the second year of the reign of Nebuchadnezzar Nebuchadnezzar dreamed dreams, wherewith his spirit was troubled, and his sleep brake from him."
(Daniel 2:1 KJV)

King Nebuchadnezzar's dream was a profound revelation concerning the kingdoms of the world all the way up through the return of Christ. This was during a time when God often spoke to mankind, including His prophets, in the form of dreams and visions. Unlike these Old Testament times, today we have our Holy Bible, and God – the Holy Spirit – speaks to us through His written Word. That is not to say that God no longer speaks to His children through dreams, but today primarily through the Scriptures. Has God ever used a dream or vision to speak directly to you? Do you hear God's voice in your heart as you read His Word? If so and you feel led, please share that experience with the class.

The Four Gentile Kingdoms
(Daniel 2:31-45)

Head of Pure Gold
Babylonian Empire
626 B.C.-539 B.C.

Chest and Arms of Silver
Media-Persian Empire
539 B.C.-331 B.C.

Belly and Thighs of Bronze
Greece-Macedonian Empire
330 B.C.-146 B.C.

Rome annexed Greece in 146 B.C.

Legs of Iron
Roman Empire
63 B.C. through the
Fall of Jerusalem in 70 A.D.

Rome added Syria & Palestine in 63 B.C.

Feet of Iron and Clay
Revised Roman Empire
"The Latter Days"
(Daniel 2:28 KJV)

Personal Experience: Ronald A. Clower

My Guardian Angel

I would like to share an experience that involves a unique relationship I have (or at least in my mind) with birds. Birds are one of God's special creations. They come in all shapes and sizes and are arrayed in a variety of stunning colors. Some are hunters feeding on the meat of their prey, while others who feed exclusively on seeds provide us with beautiful song. I have always enjoyed maintaining birdfeeders wherever we lived, just to watch and marvel at the endless activity they bring to the backyard year round. There is always drama going on, from the humming birds chasing each other around my garden, to the bluebirds residing in the birdhouses scattered throughout the backyard. Even the red-tailed hawk and the turkey vultures circling overhead provide constant entertainment – which brings me to my story.

One night many years ago I had a dream. In this dream it was revealed to me that my guardian angel would sometimes manifest himself as a red-tailed hawk. Ever since that night, I uncannily catch sight of red-tailed hawks much more frequently than I had before the dream. Sometimes they are just sitting on a wire as I pass by, but more often, I'll watch as one soars across the road in front of the truck while I'm driving. I even have a family of red-tailed hawks residing in my lower backyard. One always seems to be nearby.

One afternoon as I was strolling around the backyard, I noticed an adult red-tailed hawk circling high above me and making a great deal of racket. He continued to circle overhead as he gradually came in closer. I didn't understand what was happening, but I cautiously walked back up to the house and stood on the back porch. As I continued to watch, the hawk soared down to the ground precisely where I had been standing, picked up a large snake, and flew off. As the hawk rose higher in the air, I could plainly see at least a foot or more of snake hanging down from either side of both talons. I never saw that snake when I was standing there, but my guardian angel – a red-tailed hawk – did from high above. Now did that hawk save me from imminent danger or just happened upon another meal? I believe the Lord used that hawk not only to protect me from harm, but also to demonstrate His glory in nature through these majestic and beautiful creatures.

13

Chapter 3

The subject of chapter 3 is the decree of Nebuchadnezzar to impose universal idolatry and the resulting actions of three young Hebrew men cast into the fiery furnace when they refuse to bow to the image of gold. In the first chapter of Daniel pagan customs were judged; remember it was the diet and wisdom of the pagan world verses the Law of Moses from God. In the second chapter pagan philosophy was judged. Recall the enormous statue that represented four world kingdoms down through history – the empires of Gentile rule that became increasingly inferior to the one before and were eventually crushed by God's anointed ruler Jesus Christ. Here in chapter 3, pagan pride is judged.

The Image of Gold

3:1 – 2: "An image of gold …." This huge image illustrates an extravagant display of wealth and workmanship which went into its construction. Because of its enormity, it would not have been made of solid gold, but rather was more likely plated with gold. Nebuchadnezzar probably had this statue made in his own image; relishing the fact that Daniel had declared Nebuchadnezzar to be the head of gold in the image of his dream. Instead of humbling himself before God, the dream caused the king to be filled with extreme pride; therefore, he had the golden statue built to represent the kingdom he had built. The plain of Dura, a few miles southeast of Babylon, was flat and expansive and would allow a great multitude to assemble for worship of the image – that is the worship of the king. All the government officials were "summoned" for the dedication, and it would be their responsibility to inform the people.

Nebuchadnezzar really had three things in mind in erecting this statue:

1) The king was demonstrating his rebellion against the God of heaven who had given him world dominion. After receiving the interpretation of his dream from God through Daniel, instead of humility the king exhibited a blatant act of rebellion.
2) The statue was evidence of the king's boastful pride in making an image, which apparently was meant to exalt himself as deity.
3) The king was attempting to establish a one-world dictatorial government and religion.

3:3: When the day of dedication had arrived, all were present, except Daniel. We do not know why he was absence, the text does not say, we can only assume that he was away, most likely, on some legitimate business as chief administrator to the king of Babylon.

The KJV says, "They stood before the image …." The sight of the image of gold on the plain of Dura was very impressive – as impressive as standing at the foot of the Statue of Liberty on Ellis Island in New York Harbor or at the foot of Mount Rushmore in Keystone, South Dakota.

3:4 – 6: There was no freedom of worship at this dedication service. When the band began to play, all were "commanded" to fall down and worship the image of gold. This dedication was intended to force all the people of Babylon to worship the statue – their king. As we know, true worship (like true love) cannot be forced – it is an expression of the heart. The music was obviously used to appeal to the worldly nature of a person, that being the "flesh."

Let's touch on music for a minute: Spiritual music is a wonderful addition to worship, but sometimes today it is very difficult to distinguish between spiritual music and worldly music. The Apostle Paul wrote about the importance of music for the believer in worship. (Read Ephesians 5:19 and Colossians 3:16 out loud.) We must be cautious in our churches today; if music appeals to the flesh, then it degrades man rather than lifting him up and thus does not serve as an aid to true worship. In fact, some denominations today prohibit the use of musical instruments in their worship services for this very reason. Nevertheless, music, including the use of instruments, can in most cases elevate a worship service and be a tremendous blessing to all.

Share and discuss any personal experiences related to music in worship. Recall that Joshua heard the people singing and worshipping the golden calf and didn't know what to make of it. Moses knew what was happening and broke the stone tablets of the law (Exodus 32:17 – 19). David, on the other hand, worshipped God with music and dancing (2 Samuel 6:3 – 5). The point, with true worship, is always *who* is the object of the worship. Too often, it is us.

The king had imposed a dreadful penalty for those who refused to worship the image. The music served to assemble and prepare the people to "fall down and worship the image of gold" – everyone except, as we will see, Daniel's three young Hebrew friends.

3:7: This dedication service of the king's image, with its ritual of music, was an outward act of worship, and seemingly unanimous, for our verse reads, "all people … fell down and worshipped." There may have been many in the crowd who were not totally convinced in their hearts, but apparently they gave no visible evidence of their compromise.

3:8: The king evidently had some of his officials, astrologers or "Chaldeans" (chapter 2 verse 2), watch to see if anyone did not comply in the service. They accused the Jews. The Jews referred to here were, of course, the three Hebrew young men and friends of Daniel whom Nebuchadnezzar had appointed administrators of Babylon (2:49). There may or may not have been other Jews present at the dedication; but these three young men were in attendance because of their position in the service of the king.

3:9 – 12: The astrologers accused the three young Hebrew men before the king directly and formally and specifically by name. Their implication, "who pay no attention to you, O king," was completely false. Their refusal to worship the image was not an act of defiance towards the king; but demonstrated their recognition of a higher deity. They served and were obedient only to their God and His Word. We will see this with their reply in defense to the charges.

3:13: "Furious with rage" was the king. Here Nebuchadnezzar demonstrated a type of insanity from which he suffered. At one moment the king would be enraged and the next he would be calm or even laughing. We have seen this radical reaction before in the king (2:12).

3:14 – 15: Of these charges, the king asked, "Is it true?" Nebuchadnezzar then offered these young men the opportunity, that is, a second chance to change their minds and fall down and worship the image; while at the same time, reminding them of the penalty for refusing to do so. Though the king had heard of their God; and even experienced His power in the revealing and interpreting of his dream earlier, he was nonetheless confident that their God would not be able to deliver them from a blazing furnace.

3:16: Unlike the Chaldeans, these three Hebrews did not address the king with, "O king, live forever!" In their reply to the king, the words of these young men, "We do not need to defend ourselves," demonstrated a lack of concern or priority for their own welfare; but, more importantly it demonstrated their loyalty to the true God. They were obeying the words of God as spoken to Moses: "You shall have no other Gods before me. You shall not make for yourself an idol in the form of anything in heaven above or on the earth beneath or in the waters below. You shall not bow down to them or worship them; for I, the Lord your God, am a jealous God, punishing the children for the sins of the father to the third and fourth generation of those who hate me, but showing love to a thousand generations of those who love me and keep my commandments" (Exodus 20:3 – 6). These brave young men took a courageous stand for God.

3:17 – 18: The three Hebrews, Shadrach, Meshach, and Abednego made it perfectly clear in their reply to the king – if it was God's will, then their God could and would rescue them from the blazing furnace. They recognized God's power and trusted His sovereignty over all things. As a result, these three were determined, regardless of the consequence, to obey the Word of God and not bow down and worship the gold image of the king.

The Fiery Furnace

3:19 – 21: "Nebuchadnezzar was furious." Again, the king's uncontrollable temper is revealed. The king had his "strongest soldiers" bind the three young men and had the "fire heated seven times hotter than usual," all of this of course was not necessary; however, it did reveal the extreme emotional nature of the king's heart. The three men were then cast bound and fully clothed into the fiery furnace.

3:22 – 23: The king's urgency coupled with the extreme heat of the fire caused the soldiers (the king's strongest) to be killed by the flames; while at the same time, the three Hebrews fell headlong into the fiery furnace.

3:24 – 25: This furnace was evidently of a design and type that allowed one to observe inside of it. Nebuchadnezzar expected to watch these men be consumed immediately by the fire. However, the king leaped in amazement to not only see them alive and walking about; but also to see a fourth man, whom he described in pagan terms "like a son of the gods." Nebuchadnezzar, at that time, knew very little of the living and true God, only that Daniel had spoken of Him. The king could only testify to his unusual appearance, concluding that he was a lesser heavenly being (he referred to him as an angel in verse 28) sent by their Hebrew God. Many scholars, including myself, believe the fourth Man was the Son of God, the pre-incarnate Christ.

The deliverance of these faithful young Hebrew men from the fiery furnace was a miracle, and one of our favorite Old Testament stories of youth. There is no other explanation for what happened – you either believe it or reject it. I believe a miracle took place. I also believe the fourth Man was none other than the Lord Jesus Christ. He was present with the three Hebrew children in the furnace and He is with you and me today as we go through our trials. Read Matthew 28:20. Our Lord Jesus promises never to leave or forsake his own.

This story could also be viewed as a picture or foreshadowing of the way our Lord will provide for the believing remnant of the nation of Israel during the end-time seven-year Tribulation Period, when they refuse to worship the image of Antichrist (Revelation 12:6, 14, and 13:14 – 17).

3:26 – 27: Nebuchadnezzar acknowledged that these three young Hebrew men were "servants of the Most High God." In these first three chapters of Daniel, we have watched this king grow, a little at a time, in his knowledge of the living and true God – first with the four youths and the superiority of the Hebrew law over pagan customs (1:19), next with Daniel and his dream interpreted (2:47), and now with the deliverance of the three Hebrews from the fiery furnace. These three young men came out of the furnace completely unharmed, as noticed by the king and all his officials – not a single hair was singed nor was the smell of smoke on them. This was clearly a miracle from God.

3:28 – 30: "Praise be to the God of Shadrach, Meshach, and Abednego." Nebuchadnezzar recognized the omnipotence of the living and true God in rescuing the three from the fiery furnace. He even acknowledged that their God was superior to his and all others with the words, "for no other god can save in this way." This would become Nebuchadnezzar's conviction, as we will see later. The king gradually began abandoning the heathen practices in which he was previously engrossed while building upon his knowledge of the living and true God.

These three young Hebrew men were again back in the king's favor. Twice these young men had the decree of death upon them, and twice they had been miraculously delivered. You can even make the argument that this chapter represents the third time. The failure of the Chaldeans to interpret the king's dream in chapter 2 resulted in the first decree of death to all, including Daniel. Thus, it was Daniel's faith that asked the king for a second chance and God's deliverance which spared them. Nevertheless, each time these young men were promoted in their positions in the king's service.

Read John 10:27 – 28 and 16:33. You and I are living in a world today in which we are going to have trouble; however, God is able to keep us and bring us through them. We simply need to put our full faith and trust in the Lord, just as our three Hebrew friends did.

Review Questions

1) King Nebuchadnezzar had the enormous gold image constructed (probably in his own image) and erected, and demanded universal worship because he was filled with extreme _____.

2) The music used to call the people to assemble for worship was intended to appeal to _____

   _____.

3) The penalty for anyone who failed to fall down and worship the image was _____

   _____.

4) Daniel was probably away at this time; however, his three friends, Shadrach, Meshach, and Abednego were present at the dedication service because _____

   _____.

5) The three Hebrews refused to bow down and worship the image of the king because_____

   _____.

6) After being thrown into the fiery furnace, Nebuchadnezzar observed the three young men alive and walking alongside a fourth man whom the king referred to as "like a son of the gods." In our explanation, I suggested this fourth man was _____

   _____.

7) As a result of God's deliverance of the three Hebrews from the fiery furnace, the king acknowledged that _____.

Up for Discussion

"Therefore at that time, when all people heard the sound of the cornet, flute, harp, sackbut, psaltery, and all kind of musick, all the people, the nations, and the languages, fell down and worshipped the golden image that Nebuchadnezzar the king had set up."
(Daniel 3:7 KJV)

As we mentioned earlier in verse 7, there may have been many in the crowd – maybe even other Jews – who were not convinced, for one reason or another in their hearts; however, they gave no visible evidence of their compromise. Do you not think those Jews knew any better? Would that excuse them from God's judgment? How do we rationalize our own compromises today?

For example, your church has become increasingly liberal in recent years in its views and stances toward certain political and/or social issues with which you disagree. However, many years ago a row of pews in the church was dedicated in memory of your grandparents, and because of this you remain loyal to that church.

Another example might be a pastor who avoids preaching on certain topics because he does not fully believe the Bible's teaching on them. You continue to support him regardless.

Are you completely satisfied and in agreement with the leadership and/or message given out by your church; and if not, do you simply remain there for some other worldly reason?

Chapter 4

In this chapter we are going to learn a great deal more about this man – King Nebuchadnezzar. The many topics covered in this chapter include: 1) The personal testimony by the king, 2) The second dream of Nebuchadnezzar, 3) The interpretation of that dream by Daniel, and 4) The dream fulfilled with the king's sanity restored.

The Testimony of Nebuchadnezzar

Here begins Nebuchadnezzar's personal testimony. It shows the development in faith of this man and king. Recall from chapter 3 verse 29 the king's decree demonstrated his conviction by the Hebrew God. Now we see the king's conversion, which finally comes as a result of the experiences we will see in verses 4 – 37.

4:1 – 3: The king sent a message to "the peoples, nations and men of every language … May you prosper greatly!" The KJV reads, "Peace be multiplied unto you." Nebuchadnezzar was not speaking of peace among the nations, because he had already achieved that militarily. Instead, the king was speaking of peace of heart. This peace of which Nebuchadnezzar spoke could only come to the human heart when it knows God. The Apostle Paul tells us in Romans 5:1, "Therefore being justified by faith, we have peace with God through our Lord Jesus Christ." Only the Word of God can bring peace to the human heart, and only then can there be peace with those around us.

Nebuchadnezzar testified to God's signs, His wonders, and His dominion. The king finally recognized and acknowledged that God's rule and God's kingdom was above his. Nebuchadnezzar had finally made his peace with God. Let's watch as the king's marvelous conversion transforms him in the remaining verses.

Nebuchadnezzar's Dream of a Tree

4:4 – 5: The king continued with his message to the people, recounting the events in detail which led to his miraculous conversion. In doing so, we begin to see the first symptom of Nebuchadnezzar's alleged mental illness. If we count all the personal pronouns – I, my, and me – we see it was all about him, the king. He was full of pride, as we have already discussed. Nevertheless, based on what we have already seen in the king's behavior, doctors today might possibly classify the king's illness as hysteria, which is characterized by excitability and lack of emotional control. Does that sound familiar with this king?

4:6 – 9: As with his last dream, the king's first impulse was to call in his royal advisers; and as before, they were unable to give an interpretation of the dream. God gave Nebuchadnezzar both dreams; subsequently, only God could give the interpretation. I suspect these wise men were nothing more than a crowd of charlatans who loitered close by the king constantly feeding him morsels of pagan superstition in order to remain comfortably in his favor. In contrast, Daniel was oftentimes away, traveling throughout the kingdom seeing justifiably to the king's business. You see Daniel served God by serving the king responsibly, prudently, and with integrity. Now at last Daniel was brought before the king. Recall from chapter 1 verse 7 that Daniel was given the Babylonian name Belteshazzar, after the god Bel. Bel was another name associated with Marduk, the supreme god of the Babylonians and the king. Nevertheless, Nebuchadnezzar had remembered from his previous experience that Daniel was a man filled with the "spirit of the holy gods" – that is the Hebrew God. The king had learned that Daniel's God alone could give the correct interpretation to his dream.

4:10 – 16: These verses give us the details of the king's dream which centered on an "enormous" tree that "grew large and strong." The KJV says that this tree "reached unto heaven, and the sight thereof to the end of all the earth." It was here in Babylon (earlier called Shinar in southern Mesopotamia) that Nimrod, grandson of Ham, established the first center of his kingdom and began to build "a tower that reaches to the heavens …" (Genesis 11:4). Recall the Lord put an end to that prideful construction project by confusing their language and causing the people to scatter over the face of the earth.

Our Scriptures have oftentimes used a tree as a descriptive metaphor. In Psalm 1:2 – 3, a tree was compared to a man whose "delight is in the law of the Lord." A tree has also been used to represent a nation, as with Assyria in Ezekiel 31:3 – 14 and the nation of Israel in Matthew 24:32 – 33. Our Lord Jesus Christ used the mustard tree in Matthew 13:31 – 32 to represent Christian growth today and the Apostle Paul used the olive tree in Romans 11:16 – 24 to represent both Israel and the Gentiles. The enormous tree here represents Nebuchadnezzar and his great world empire. It was from him and his boundless kingdom that all "creatures" subsisted.

The "messenger, a holy one," mentioned in verse 13, refers to an angel. Angels are a heavenly order of created beings who administer the will of God in the world and His universe. At the command of this angel, the tree was cut down and its stump and roots bound. The fact that it was bound and allowed to "remain in the ground," suggests that the tree would be released to flourish again someday. Also worth noting here in verse 15 is that the symbolism changes from that of a tree to a man, for the text reads, "Let him be drenched with the dew of heaven …."

So much are the mind and the heart interwoven in man that the NIV text of verse 16 reads "Let his mind be changed from that of a man and let him be given the mind of an animal"; whereby the KJV says, "Let his heart be changed …." Regardless, the suggestion here is that this great and mighty ruler was to be changed in character from a man into a beast "till seven times pass by for him." In Scripture, seven is God's number for completeness. The word "times" probably means years, since Daniel used the same word elsewhere in later chapters when referring to a three and a half year period in the future (7:25 and 12:7). Thus, for seven years the king would be transformed and reduced to life spent amongst the animals and plants of the earth.

4:17: This one verse is the key to the whole chapter. Here are the three things we are to learn from Nebuchadnezzar's dream:

1) "The Most High is sovereign over the kingdoms of men." We mentioned this back in our introduction as the primary theme of the Book of Daniel. God is sovereign and is in complete control. He has not abandoned His people or this world, though He does allow Satan certain latitudes as He purposes. Nations and empires rise and kingdoms fall to teach men that God rules "over the kingdoms of men."

2) God "gives them to anyone he wishes." Political parties do not put men in power, God does. Some leaders may even boast in their God-given position of power; but, I would caution them. God disposes of kings and kingdoms according to His and only His will. The Apostle Paul wrote: "Everyone must submit himself to the governing authorities, for there is no authority except that which God has established. The authorities that exist have been established by God" (Romans 13:1).

3) God "sets over them the lowliest of men." This statement should be humbling to us all. In our democracy today, we rarely pick the best man for the office; but oftentimes, God gives us precisely what we deserve. The head of gold, Nebuchadnezzar, suffered from mental illness; yet he was a brilliant ruler who built the first great world empire. History has continued to record down through the years the rise and fall of the powerful, many suffering from similar problems such as this king.

4:18: The king had completed his description of the dream, and he was fully confident in Daniel's ability to interpret it. Nebuchadnezzar knew that Daniel was filled with the Spirit of God, and he now hoped, or expected to hear another lofty revelation concerning him from God.

Daniel Interprets the Dream

4:19: "Then Daniel was greatly perplexed …." Daniel was shocked because the message he received from God was one of judgment. You see, Nebuchadnezzar and Daniel had become close colleagues; and for that reason, Daniel was hesitant to reveal its meaning to the king. Daniel wished that the dream would somehow apply to the king's enemies instead. Yet Daniel, in the end, was truthful with his friend and king.

4:20 – 22: The tree represented Nebuchadnezzar. The king with his kingdom had grown strong and become great. The "beautiful leaves and abundant fruit" represent the provision of abundant blessings for all, and the beasts and birds represent the happy citizens of his kingdom. He had become the ruler of the known civilized world. The tree represented the king and his dominion.

4:23 – 24: The tree was to be cut off, but not uprooted; in other words, Nebuchadnezzar would be deposed, but not rejected. For seven years, the king was to live "like the wild animals" of the field. The phrase "drenched with the dew of heaven" may be a reference to some change in the king's appearance, or it may simply mean that, in his insanity, Nebuchadnezzar didn't have the sense to come in out of the rain, much less to come inside to sleep. This "decree" or judgment was from the true God in heaven.

4:25 – 26: Daniel was trying to explain to Nebuchadnezzar why the dream applied to him. Nebuchadnezzar was filled with extreme pride and arrogance, taking full credit for the glory and majesty that was his. This was evident when he had the enormous image of himself built and forced everyone in his kingdom to fall down and worship it [him]. Now God was going to humble him. The king was to be driven out of his palace and into the fields where he would live with the wild animals. Nebuchadnezzar's insanity would literally cause him to believe himself to be an animal, and his affliction would run for seven years. In the end, the king would learn and finally "acknowledge that the Most High" – the true God in "Heaven" – rules over the kingdoms of men. Only then was God willing to restore the king's sanity along with his crown.

Let's take a quick biblical look at the sin of pride. God hates all sin, but pride is the one sin that seems to be characteristic of most, if not all men. Pride is the favored sin Satan uses to attack you and me. It is the beginning of all other sin. But what do we have to be proud of? Read what the prophet says in Jeremiah 9:23 – 24.

There is absolutely no room for pride in God's plan of salvation for mankind. When we come to Christ for salvation, we can only do so humbly, stripped of self, and completely void of pride. In 1 Corinthians 2:2, the Apostle Paul tells us: "For I resolved to know nothing while I was with you except Jesus Christ and him crucified." In 1 Corinthians 4:7, he continues with the following: "For who makes you different from anyone else? What do you have that you did not receive? And if you did receive it, why do you boast as though you did not?" Finally, the apostle writes, "Let him who boasts boast in the Lord" (2 Corinthians 10:17).

God hates pride so much that He put it number one on His hate list: "These six things doth the Lord hate; yea, seven are an abomination unto him: A proud look, a lying tongue, and hands that shed innocent blood" (Proverbs 6:16 – 17 KJV).

Last and most importantly, it was our Lord Jesus Christ who gave us the finest example of humility, as elegantly written by the Apostle Paul: "And being found in the appearance of a man, he humbled himself and became obedient to death even death on a cross!" (Philippians 2:8).

4:27: King Nebuchadnezzar, the ruler of the known world, was overwhelmed by pride and therefore was living in sin. Because of this looming judgment, Daniel felt compelled to encourage the king to repent and rule his kingdom in righteousness. Maybe then he would avoid the coming judgment and the king would know the true peace of God. I think this was God's final warning to Nebuchadnezzar.

The Dream Comes to Pass

4:28 – 30: Nebuchadnezzar chose not to follow Daniel's advice. God even gave the king a one-year grace period before His judgment fell upon him. How gracious and patient God was!

Daniel had already revealed the king's dream and told Nebuchadnezzar that his kingdom was given to him by the Most High God. The king was to acknowledge that truth, otherwise judgment would come. Despite his best counsel, the king in all his pride and arrogance looked out from his palace roof and made the following statement: "Is not this the great Babylon I have built …." The contrast to this statement will be found in verse 37 which we will see shortly.

4:31 – 33: While the king's words were "still on his lips," the foretold judgment was declared and brought down in full upon the king directly by God. The king's sanity slipped away, along with his kingdom, as he was driven out into the fields to eat grass and live amongst the wild animals. In those days, the insane were driven out rather than being placed in some institution for treatment. Daniel knew fully the king's dream, and thus understood that his judgment was only temporary and that the king would one day be restored in both his sanity and his position as king. Moreover, I believe Daniel, being second to the king (2:48), likely assumed responsibility and administered the affairs of the kingdom righteously during the time of the king's affliction. A situation such as this would not normally allow a king to return to the throne; yet, God promised Nebuchadnezzar that he would do so after he had humbled himself and acknowledged that God was sovereign.

4:34: At the end of the seven years the king raised his "eyes toward heaven," not toward some idol or heathen temple as before, but to the one true God who resides in heaven. His sanity was restored and he "praised the Most High … who lives forever."

Recall Nebuchadnezzar's testimony that we began reading at the opening of this chapter. His testimony resulted from the experiences described in this chapter. Here, in these closing verses, the king continued in his dialogue of praise to the Most High God whose "dominion is eternal … and endures from generation to generation."

4:35: Nebuchadnezzar had learned that the Most High God was sovereign and in complete control of "heaven" and "earth" – the universe. The king had learned his lesson well and accepted his discipline as God's will for him, surrendering his prideful heart and mind to the sovereignty of God.

4:36 – 37: Nebuchadnezzar's sanity was restored. His officials, led by Daniel, gathered around him and his honor and position as King of Babylon was reinstated. The kingdom was never in danger or at risk during the long period of the king's absence; in fact the text said that it "became even greater than before." The king's conversion to and knowledge of the one true and living God was complete, for he no longer called God "the God of Shadrach, Meshach, and Abednego" (3:28); but from then on, King Nebuchadnezzar referred to God as "the Most High" and "the King of heaven" (4:34 and 37).

Review Questions

1) Nebuchadnezzar was full of pride which led to a mental condition which we suggested was

_____.

2) The king believed Daniel could interpret his dream because he believed Daniel was filled with

_____.

3) The messengers or holy ones mentioned in verse 17 were _____.

4) List the three key things we are to learn from this chapter: _____

_____.

5) The enormous tree in the king's dream represented _____.

6) God's judgment resulting in the king's insanity lasted seven years until the king finally acknowledged that _____.

7) The king's acknowledgment completed his conversion and he now referred to God as _____

_____.

Up for Discussion

"The Most High ruleth in the kingdom of men, and giveth to whomever he will,
and setteth up over it the basest of men."
(Daniel 4:17 KJV)

I made the statement in our study above of verse 17, that in our democracy today, we rarely pick the best man for the office; but oftentimes, God gives us precisely what we deserve. Both biblical and secular history has recorded countless times down through the years the rise and fall of powerful men, many of whom suffered similarly as Nebuchadnezzar with disorders associated with mental illness. One example that immediately comes to mind is Israel's first monarch, Saul. He rose from humble beginnings to become Israel's first king but was deposed by God for his unfaithfulness resulting from extreme pride and intense jealousy, neither of which he could control.

I would suggest that any leader who feels empowered enough to oppress his people in order to elevate his own status and indulgence, or persecute them for expressing an opinion contrary to his own suffers from a form of insanity. It is not sane for a ruler to tax his people into poverty so that he may live in utmost luxury as was the case in first century Galilee and modern-day North Korean. Is insanity, thus a demon deposited by Satan into a person once he finds a weakness and establishes a foothold in that life? Take a look at world history, or even our own nation's history; cite some examples that would demonstrate the rise of a powerful leader and the alleged insanity which led to their eventual downfall.

Discuss or consider how this example of God's judgment and restoration might also represent an instructive "type" or example for both the nation of Israel and the unrepentant sinner.

Ronald A. Clower

Personal Experience: Warren W. Huddleston
Senior Pastor Dallas First United Methodist Church
Dallas, Georgia

A Vision of Judgment

A vision is totally different than a dream. Dreams occur when we are asleep and sometimes we even know we are asleep. A vision occurs when we know we are awake, at least at the beginning. It is the state the mind is in that is different than any other time. During the two visions I have had, I know nothing else mattered at the time. I also know that Peter in Acts 2:17 said, "I will pour out of my Spirit upon all flesh: and your sons and your daughters shall prophesy, and your young men shall see visions, and your old men shall dream dreams."

The vision I had some years ago when I was sixteen, happened when I was in a car accident. I was on my way home from school in my little VW Beetle. It was raining and I was driving too fast. The highway ahead was very curvy and I lost control. With slick tires on the back, I began to slide and felt like I was skating on ice. I realized I was headed straight toward a utility pole. In a panic, I turned the steering wheel to miss the pole, but my right front tire hit the shoulder of the road in such a way as it caused the car to flip onto its left side. I was now laying on the driver's door as the car slid about 200 yards before finally coming to a stop.

I lay there in the car stunned by all that I had just seen, and I am not talking about the wreck. For during the thirty seconds that the wreck had taken, I had seen a vision. The Apostle Paul wrote: "We shall all stand before the judgment seat of Christ" (Romans 14:10). During this wreck I had stood there. The vision was quite simple but yet very complex. I stood before God, the Holy Spirit. He said, "Look at this with Me." I viewed my whole life. The vision started with a two or three year old little boy. Every word, every thought, everything I had ever done was shown me. It was like I watched my whole life as I had lived it standing before God. Nothing was left out. I remembered everything I saw. I remembered doing it all. It was me. I could not hide one thing. My spirit stood with God's Spirit and we viewed my life pure and simple. When we came to the wreck, I saw all the fear that my subconscious had experienced, but was not aware of it. That was what brought me to this place. I actually thought I was going to die. The Spirit told me He was sending me back because I was not ready to come there yet. I told Him I would do better because now I understood what Jesus meant when He said, "I say unto you, that every idle word that men shall speak, they shall give account thereof in the Day of Judgment" (Matthew 12:36).

I wish I could tell you this changed me completely until this day, but I cannot. When I think over the years that have passed since the accident, I cringe at some of the things I have said and done, even more so what I have thought. I would like to make one point clear. As I watched my life with God, the Spirit, I did not feel condemned. I felt and heard Him say every time I committed a sin, "I forgive you because of your belief in my Son, Jesus." Over and over I heard this. He smiled at some things and I remembered He laughed once. I was so glad He said He was sending me back. More quickly than I had left, I was back in my car.

Since this has happened to me, I have not been afraid of dying. I am not saying I am ready to stand before God and view my life; but, I am saying I know He does not condemn me. For if this vision taught me anything, it taught me God loves me and He forgives me through Jesus' blood. Based on this I am not afraid of death.

"O death, where is thy sting? O grave, where is thy victory?"
(I Corinthians 15:55 KJV)

Chapter 5

In this chapter Daniel, continuing his chronicles of Babylonian history, has fast-forwarded in time to the final days of this great empire and its ultimate downfall as a result of the judgment of God upon its last ruler. Who is this King Belshazzar? Subject wise, we will look at his feast of revelry, the handwriting of God on the wall, the wise men's failure to read it, Daniel's interpretation of the handwriting, and its fulfillment resulting in the fall of Babylon.

The Feast of Revelry

5:1: "King Belshazzar …." This king's name, Belshazzar, means "Bel (Babylon's chief god), protect the king." This figure had once been the source of historical controversy since most scholars concluded there was no such king, thus lending question to Daniel's validity. However, further research, based on the Nabonidus Cylinder and other sources, revealed that the name Bel-shar-usur (Belshazzar) had been found on clay cylinders in which he was called the son of Nabonidus. Additionally, it was believed that Nabonidus, the last king of the Babylonian Empire, spent a great deal of time away from the kingdom with his army, and his son, Belshazzar, remained behind in Babylon serving as viceroy. Later in verse 22, he is referred to as the "son" of Nebuchadnezzar; but since Daniel was then writing in Aramaic, that term could have also meant "descendant" or relative of. King Nabonidus was the son-in-law of Nebuchadnezzar, thus making Belshazzar Nebuchadnezzar's grandson. Consequently, Belshazzar's position was "second" highest in the kingdom.

Pride and arrogance was characteristic of this man as well. He "gave a great banquet for a thousand of his nobles" at the same time that Gobryas, the Median general, was laying siege to the city outside. This was confirmed by the Greek historians, Herodotus and Xenophon. They described how the city was easily conquered by cutting off and rerouting of a channel from the Euphrates River that brought water into the city so that the Mede armies could simply march underneath the walls in its place. Belshazzar arrogantly believed the city was impenetrable and secure to hold such an excessive event in the face of the enemy right outside the walls. His defiance to the enemy, though blatant, was dangerously naïve and, as we will see, resulted in his death and the downfall of the great Babylonian Empire.

5: 2 – 4: Not only did this man defy the enemy outside besieging the city, but in the presence of his guests and under the influence of wine, he dishonored his grandfather by blaspheming God.

Nebuchadnezzar was indeed a young heathen king when he destroyed Jerusalem and took the gold and silver vessels from the temple; however, he later came to acknowledge the one true living God – praising and honoring Him as the Most High – as we learned from our previous chapter. After his conversion, Nebuchadnezzar likely had the temple vessels stored away for safe keeping. Belshazzar knew all of this (verse 22), yet deliberately ordered the vessels brought out to be used in a drunken orgy to toast their heathen gods. This second act of defiance, to the true God and God of his grandfather, demonstrated the immaturity and foolishness of this young ruler.

The Handwriting of God on the Wall

5:5: This irreverent insult to heaven and to the God of his grandfather resulted in an immediate response from God. God did not wish to speak to this man in a dream nor convert him as He did with his grandfather. God was incensed! Then, without hesitancy, God directly proclaimed judgment upon this man by writing on the wall of the banquet hall in His own divine hand. Let me suggest that this visible "human hand" that wrote on the plaster wall belonged to that of the same person we saw back in chapter 3, that fourth person Nebuchadnezzar observed in the fiery furnace with the three Hebrews – the Son of God, the pre-incarnate Christ. This decree from God was written "near the lampstand" so that all who were present, especially this brazen king, could plainly see it.

5:6 – 7: Belshazzar's "face turned pale." This supernatural proclamation from God, though sobering I'm sure, was so devastatingly frightening to this man that he could not stand upright on his own two feet, for our text tells us, "his legs gave way." The king called for his "wise men" and offered a reward to anyone who could interpret the writing. The reward would include being made "third highest" in the kingdom. Nabonidus, the real king, was away with his army and Belshazzar, his son, was ruling as "second" in the kingdom. This simple truth demonstrates the accuracy of Daniel's writing, and proves that he was present and well aware of the state of affairs within the kingdom at that time.

5:8 – 9: The wise men of Babylon were brought in before the king and asked to interpret the writing. Though the reward was attractive, these royal advisers, as in times before, were unable to give any interpretation. This is the third time in our study that we have witnessed the failure of these wise men to answer their king's command for an explanation. The mood of the banquet, for both Belshazzar and his guests, had now changed from that of revelry to one of terror and confusion.

5:10: "The queen …." This is likely Nebuchadnezzar's wife, Amytis, who is now the "queen mother" and Belshazzar's grandmother. It could also be alleged that she was the daughter of Nebuchadnezzar and wife of Nabonidus, the current king. Nevertheless, she apparently overheard the uproar taking place in the banquet hall and went in to inspect and offer assistance to the king.

5:11 – 12: The queen mother had come in to comfort her grandson and suggest an alternative solution. In describing Daniel, the queen used the same expression Nebuchadnezzar used: A man "who has the spirit of the holy gods in him" (4:8, 9, and 18). His grandfather, the king, she continued to explain, had found him to be a wise and Spirit-filled man and, as a result, had appointed him chief over all the wise men of Babylon (2:48). The queen mother's confidence in Daniel was born out of her earlier experiences when her husband, Nebuchadnezzar was king. She then assured Belshazzar that Daniel possessed exceptional "knowledge and understanding" and could indeed interpret the writing. "Call for Daniel" was her advice.

5:13 – 14: Apparently Belshazzar did not know Daniel. Daniel evidently had been relieved of his high office or moved into a less prominent position of service after the death of Nebuchadnezzar in 562 B.C. The year was 539 B.C., and Daniel had grown to be an old man around eighty years of age when brought before this king.

5:15 – 16: Belshazzar explained to Daniel that his wise men were unable to interpret the writing. The king also made reference to earlier instances when he had heard of Daniel's abilities to "solve difficult problems" in an attempt, I believe, to flatter him and encourage his willingness to help. The king lastly offered Daniel the same reward he offered to his wise men, including being made "third highest ruler in the kingdom."

5:17: Daniel refused the king's gifts and reward not only because he had no desire or use for them; but also because Daniel well understood that the kingdom was on the verge of collapse. The city was under siege by the Mede armies. Despite this, he agreed to interpret the writing; but before doing so, Daniel gave this young ruler, Belshazzar, the only Sunday school lesson he had ever received.

5:18 – 19: Daniel explained to Belshazzar that God had made his grandfather, Nebuchadnezzar, ruler of the known world and the greatest king ever to rule over men – with "sovereignty and greatness and glory and splendor." Daniel continued with his lesson by recounting the humbling experience Nebuchadnezzar was given by God.

5:20 – 24: Daniel's lesson to Belshazzar was direct and powerful. God had given Nebuchadnezzar complete and absolute sovereignty over the kingdoms of men; but, when his heart became "arrogant and hardened with pride," God humbled him. Daniel reminded Belshazzar of the tragic and humiliating ordeal that his grandfather had experienced for seven years. Belshazzar had heard all these stories and knew well of his grandfather's insanity and how it was restored along with his throne once he acknowledged that the Most High God was sovereign over the kingdoms of men. However, prideful as he was, Belshazzar failed to learn from his grandfather's experience.

God hardens the heart and brings into judgment those who have been shown the truth but reject it. It will be the same for those who reject the gospel during the Tribulation Period of the latter days. The Apostle Paul explains, "The coming of the lawless one will be in accordance with the work of Satan displayed in all kinds of counterfeit miracles, signs, and wonders, and in every sort of evil that deceives those who are perishing. They perish because they refuse to love the truth and so be saved. For this reason God sends them a powerful delusion so that they will believe the lie and so that all will be condemned who have not believed the truth but have delighted in wickedness" (2 Thessalonians 2:9 – 12). You see, when you reject the truth, you are wide open to the lies from all the cults, isms, and charlatans of the world.

Belshazzar's first sin was his willful and arrogant pride. This pride led to his other sins – he mocked and blasphemed God by desecrating the sacred vessels taken from the Lord's temple in Jerusalem then used them to praise their heathen gods. Daniel concluded his lesson by telling Belshazzar that the hand was sent by God whom he, the king, had scorned and blasphemed.

Daniel Interprets the Handwriting

5:25 – 28: Daniel read the handwriting: "MENE, MENE, TEKEL, UPHARIN" (KJV).

MENE can mean mina (a unit of money) or numbered, and here it was repeated for emphasis. God had numbered the days of Belshazzar's reign (and that of the great Babylonian Empire) and its time was up.

God is omniscient – He has infinite knowledge – He is all-knowing – and only God knows the number of days we have on this earthly plain until our time is also up. The psalmist reminds us to pray that God would: "Teach us to number our days aright, that we may gain a heart of wisdom" (Psalm 90:12).

TEKEL can mean shekel or weighed. God had weighed Belshazzar's kingdom on his divine scale and had found it wanting; in other words, it had not measured up to the standards of God's righteousness. Even today, we would fail to measure up to God's standards based on our good deeds alone, for the prophet wrote: "And all our righteous acts are like filthy rags" (Isaiah 64:6). The only way we can measure up to God is through a personal relationship with His Son Jesus Christ. The Apostle Paul clarified this simple truth: "This righteousness from God comes through faith in Jesus Christ to all who believe. There is no difference, for all have sinned and fall short of the glory of God, and are justified freely by his grace through the redemption that came by Jesus Christ" (Romans 3:22 – 24).

God weighs each and every one of us simply on the basis of our acceptance or our rejection of His precious Son, Jesus Christ.

UPHARIN (AND PARSIN) can mean a half mina or divided or Persia (similarly spelled). UPHARSIN is the plural of PERES that we find in verse 28. The kingdom of Babylon would be divided and given to the Medes and Persians. History confirms that on "that very night" the great city of Babylon, under the co-regency of Nabonidus and Belshazzar was in fact conquered by the Medes and Persians.

God is sovereign and in complete control of the kingdoms of earth, and He will continue to establish and remove kingdoms until Christ returns to earth to set up His eternal kingdom.

5:29: Daniel was awarded the royal gifts and made "third highest ruler in the kingdom" (as short-lived as it was). As I mentioned back in verse 7, this fact confirmed the accuracy of Daniel's writing at the time. Nabonidus was the true king, and Belshazzar was his son and co-regent, and therefore was merely second in command.

5:30 – 31: "That very night …." As I mentioned earlier, while the banquet was in full swing, the Mede armies were marching underneath the walls of the city where their water supply had been cut off and channeled away. The Greek historian, Xenophon, recorded that the armies of General Gobryas were well into the inner city before the palace guards had become aware of anything wrong. With little resistance, the kingdom was conquered and its king, Belshazzar was slain.

The Prophet Isaiah foretold the fall of Babylon (Isaiah 21:1 – 10) and prophesied the rise of Cyrus the Persian who united the Medes and Persians in order to conquer Babylon (Isaiah 41:2).

"Darius the Mede took over the kingdom." The name Darius here could be the throne name in Babylon taken by the Persian emperor Cyrus the Great; but it is unlikely that Cyrus would be called a "Mede" since he was first and foremost a Persian. More likely, Darius was another name for Gubaru, the governor newly appointed by Cyrus to rule over the conquered Babylonian territories. The head of pure gold, Babylon had been removed. The chest and arms of silver, the Media-Persian Empire then began its period of rule (reference from chapter 2).

In "the latter days" another Babylon, a revised kingdom, will also fall by the hand of God (Revelation, chapter 18); and this will finally bring an end to man's exalted rule on earth.

The Handwriting on the Wall (Daniel 5:25)

MENE, MENE, TEKEL, UPHARSIN

Review Questions

1) King Belshazzar was related in what way to Nebuchadnezzar? _____.

2) Who was the actual king at the time? _____.

3) What was going on behind the scenes during the king's banquet? _____

_____.

4) What was King Belshazzar's first sin? _____.

5) What other sins did this lead the king into? _____

_____.

6) Daniel's interpretation of the handwriting revealed for the kingdom of Babylon the following: Its days had been _____; it had been _____ and found lacking according to God's standards; and it would be _____ and given over to another empire.

7) God's judgment upon this king and his kingdom came to pass on _____.

Up for Discussion

"And thou his son, O Belshazzar, hast not humbled thine heart,
though thou knewest all this." (Daniel 5:22 KJV)

This verse, spoken by Daniel in his little Sunday school lesson to Belshazzar, confirms that this young king remembered well the stories about his grandfather, Nebuchadnezzar, and how his experiences had brought him to the knowledge of the one true living God. Nebuchadnezzar had learned to praise and glorify the Most High who lives forever; and as a result, God had restored him into an even greater king. However, Belshazzar failed to learn from his grandfather's experiences. His youthful pride led him down his own path; one that not only proved to be foolish, but also led to his own demise and the downfall of his kingdom.

Speaking for myself, I can recall at least two occasions in my early professional career when I ignored the advice of my parents, believing at the time that I knew better than they what I was doing. This was also at a time when I did not seek God in prayer before making major business decisions. The result each time was devastating – emotionally and financially. I not only lost a great deal of money, but each time also cost me a close friend – one I am estranged from still today.

Why do you suppose youth oftentimes chooses to ignore the voice of experience? Is it simply pride that causes them to want to forge their own path, or is it something else? If you feel comfortable enough, please share with the class an experience where you would have fared a much better outcome had you listened and taken the advice of someone older and more experienced; or had you taken the matter to God in prayer.

The Hand Writing on the Wall (Daniel 5:25)

מְנֵא מְנֵא תְּקֵל פַּרְסִין

Chapter 6

This chapter is one of the most familiar in all of Scripture. It takes us back to those early days of our youth, while sitting on the rug in our Sunday school classroom around our teacher as she read those endless stories of faith and God's love for His children – this is certainly one of our favorites. This is the story of Daniel in the lions' den. Here we will see, as I mentioned in our introduction, that Daniel was a man of prayer – always giving thanks to his God; and this man of prayer would embrace a faith so strong and so extraordinary that it would proof to be his ultimate deliverance.

This chapter is a companion to chapter 3 where God safely delivered Daniel's three friends from the fiery furnace. Likewise, this story could also be viewed as a picture or foreshadowing of the way our Lord will provide for the believing remnant of the nation of Israel (and the Gentiles) during the seven-year Tribulation Period, when they refuse to worship the image of Antichrist (Revelation 12:6, 14, and 13:14 – 17).

The late J. Vernon McGee associated this story with an interesting analogy he left for us today. He compared the world around us to that of a lion's cage, and said the message for us is found in the words of the apostle: "Be self-controlled and alert. Your enemy the devil prowls around like a roaring lion looking for someone to devour" (1 Peter 5:8). How remarkable was his insight!

6:1 – 2: We have moved ahead in history into a new kingdom, the Media-Persian Empire, represented by the chest and arms of silver in Nebuchadnezzar's dream of chapter 2. As mentioned in chapter 5, Darius the Mede was likely another name for Gubaru, the governor newly appointed by Cyrus, King of Persia to rule over the conquered Babylonian territories, including Syria, Phoenicia, and Palestine. The fact that he was referred to as "king" throughout this chapter was not necessarily an inaccuracy, despite being a subordinate to Cyrus. In the same manner, Belshazzar was referred to as king even though he was second in command of Babylon under his father Nabonidus.

Taken from our discussion of chapter 2, the diminishing value of the metal from one kingdom to the next (head of gold to chest and arms of silver) symbolically suggests a decrease in the absolute power and authority of its ruler. This fact immediately becomes apparent in these opening verses. Nebuchadnezzar shared his authority with no one – his rule was solitary and absolute. In contrast, Darius "appointed 120 satraps," or "princes" (KJV), and three administrators, or "presidents" (KJV) over them, thus establishing a delegation of authority. In the ancient world, as today, corruption in government was widespread. For the king, "not suffer loss" would refer to taxes; and it was thus the responsibility of these three administrators to ensure the satraps not fall into corruption and thievery. Darius apparently saw something special in Daniel to have appointed him one of these top administrators in his newly formed government.

6:3: Remember, Daniel was around eighty years old at that time, and likely the eldest among Darius' royal officials. Daniel possessed "exceptional qualities," or as the KJV states "an excellent spirit." We have mentioned many times thus far that Daniel was a "Spirit-filled" man. Daniel's proficiency and integrity in his work was unequaled, and Darius took note of him. The king had such confidence in Daniel that he "set him over the whole kingdom," meaning Darius made Daniel second only to himself in power and authority.

6:4: Daniel then held the top administrative position in Darius' government, and as a result, the other "administrators and satraps" exhibited a jealous spirit towards Daniel. This is still true today. If you are at the top of your profession, then there will always be those under you who will watch and try to find a flaw or weakness in you that they can exploit for their own selfish gain. In Daniel's case, his long life and career of government service was without blemish – they could find nothing in his conduct, past or present, to bring charge against.

As Christians, we should strive to live our lives in the same way. Human nature is such that people will always talk about you behind your back; but you can live your life so as to prove them to be right on the positive things they say and liars on the bad things. We should take to heart the words of the Apostle Paul: "Do everything without complaining or arguing, so that you may become blameless and pure children of God without fault in a crooked and depraved generation, in which you shine like stars in the universe" (Philippians 2:14).

6:5: Daniel's character was quite contrary to the others and they well understood that. Daniel was a devout man of God and his prayer life was well known to them. Thus, Daniel's only vulnerability, as they saw it, would lie in his religion, and so it was there that they sought to create a conflict between the king and Daniel. They knew Daniel would always follow the law of his God over the law of man.

6:6 – 9: The conspiracy of the administrators and satraps against Daniel was two-fold. First, they took advantage of the king by playing to his (and every king's) weakness – his vanity. They addressed the king with, "O King Darius, live forever," and then suggested that he issue a decree forcing everyone to pray only to him during the following thirty days or suffer penalty of death. The second thing these conspirators did was lie to the king. They stated that "all" the king's administrators and advisors agreed with the proposed decree, knowing well that Daniel, the king's top administrator, was completely unaware of the proposal. Darius yielded to their flattery and signed the decree which then could not be changed.

The Prayer of Daniel

6:10: Daniel only learned of the king's decree after it "had been published." Daniel's reaction to the king's new law was one of non-compromise – God's law was greater than man's. The fact that his windows were "opened toward Jerusalem" did not demonstrate defiance to the king on Daniel's part, but was simply a matter consistent with his usual prayer life. At that time, it was the Jewish requirement that if you were away from the temple in Jerusalem, then you were to pray facing that direction. Daniel was a man of prayer and he had no intention of changing his beliefs and practices because of Darius' decree. He prayed toward Jerusalem and he prayed three times a day, "giving thanks to his God." David, the psalmist wrote: "Evening, morning and noon I cry out in distress, and he hears my voice" (Psalm 55:17).

6:11: Daniel had a reputation of being a committed man of prayer; subsequently, his conspirators were correct in their assumption that Daniel would undoubtedly choose his God over any earthly king to whom to pray. Daniel asked "God for help" – he made "supplication before his God." This meant Daniel faithfully placed the matter in God's hands. As was the case with his three friends and the fiery furnace (chapter 3), Daniel also trusted that if it was God's will, then He could and would rescue him.

Do you think that the reference to the open windows facing Jerusalem indicates that Daniel was praying in private, not in public? Daniel was not forcing his religion on others, but he was committed to observing it privately as God directed. Consequently, in order for the accusation to be made, the conspirators had to spy on him, watching and listening to Daniel pray in private from outside his home.

6:12 – 15: The conspirators immediately reported Daniel's disobedience to the king – "He still prays three times a day," they said. To emphasize their accusation, they referred to Daniel not as the king's chief administrator, but as "one of the exiles from Judah." This news "greatly distressed" Darius because Daniel was his top and most trusted advisor, and likely a close friend as well. Unfortunately, the law could not be changed. It is worth noting that had Nebuchadnezzar been king, then I believe he would have been able to change the law in order to rescue his friend. Darius acted "in accordance with the laws of the Medes and Persians." This again showed the deterioration in authority of the ruler from one empire to the next. Darius could do nothing to prevent Daniel from being thrown into the lions' den.

Daniel in the Lions' Den

6:16: The word den in Aramaic means "pit." Daniel was thrown into a pit full of lions – hungry lions I am sure. The kings of Assyria kept lions in captivity and released them from time to time for the royal sport of lion hunting. King Darius probably kept these lions for the same purpose. It is suggested that these dens were so constructed with a small opening at the top, since lions were unable to climb. In addition, there was a small side opening through which the beasts were admitted and released. This may have been the "mouth" or entrance that was used to thrust Daniel into the den.

Daniel's life and close service to two world rulers proved to be a tremendous testimony and witness to the saving grace of God. King Darius had begun to learn, as did Nebuchadnezzar that Daniel's God was all-powerful, and if He wished so could deliver Daniel. Darius recognized Daniel's faithfulness to his God with the words, "your God, whom you serve continually." In the same manner, the Apostle Paul wrote the following to encourage us today to live a life of faithfulness: "Therefore, my dear brothers, stand firm. Let nothing move you. Always give yourselves fully to the work of the Lord, because you know that your labor in the Lord is not in vain" (1 Corinthians 15:58).

6:17: A stone was laid over the mouth of the den and sealed with the king's "own signet ring" and with the "rings of his nobles" to ensure that no one intervened on Daniel's behalf. Daniel spent the night with a pack of wild and fierce lions; after all, lions are by nature nocturnal, hunting and feeding at night.

6:18 – 20: Darius could not sleep. He was so distressed that he spent the night alone, sleepless, and in anguish over concern for his trusted companion Daniel. At the break of dawn, the king "hurried to the lions' den" and cried out to his friend Daniel. In his plea, Darius now referred to Daniel's God as the "living God." The king's faith in Daniel's God was coming around; yet at this point, we are not certain if the king really expected Daniel to answer – but Daniel did.

6:21 – 22: "O king, live forever!" This was the standard manner in which to greet a king, but here it may also have served as a blessing from Daniel to King Darius. To live forever was only possible through an acknowledgment of Daniel's God – the one, true living God and source of life. Daniel trusted in God's power and sovereignty over all things; and thus, his deliverance from the lions' den was another miracle, just as his three friends were delivered safely from the fiery furnace. I believe the "angel" God sent to "shut the mouths of the lions" was again the same as Nebuchadnezzar saw inside the fiery furnace – the Son of God, the pre-incarnate Christ.

6:23: Darius was very fond of Daniel and was extremely "overjoyed" that he had survived a night amongst the lions. It was Daniel's faithfulness that got him sentenced to death, but it was his faith that saved him from the jaws of death. The writer of Hebrews celebrated the glories attributed to God through faith as demonstrated by Old Testament Patriarchs when he wrote: "Who through faith conquered kingdoms, administered justice, and gained what was promised; who shut the mouths of lions" (Hebrews 11:33).

6:24: After Daniel was removed, the conspirators, along with their families, were thrown into the lions' den. I mentioned above that these lions were wild and fierce, and here we see that horribly demonstrated. The "wives and children" were included in this dreadful death sentence because the Persians, like the Hebrews at times (Joshua 7:19 – 26), considered guilt a shared responsibility among family members. This "guilt by association" was in accordance with the principle of corporate solidarity and was a common custom held by many other nations at the time as well.

6:25 – 27: The king's original thirty-day decree by then had likely expired. Here, Darius issued a new decree and one that also served as his personal testimony. He began it with the very same words that Nebuchadnezzar (4:1) used, "Peace be multiplied unto you" (KJV). You see, Darius had found the same peace that Nebuchadnezzar found so many years before. The king commanded all people to fear and revere "the God of Daniel." Darius had now come around completely to the knowledge of the one, true "living God;" and, in his new decree, testified to God's awesome power and enduring sovereignty.

6:28: "Daniel prospered" and remained in the king's service until the end of his life which came during the reign of Cyrus. Darius served Cyrus for little more than a year, until which time Cyrus appointed his son Cambyses II as vice-regent over the Babylonian territories. Cyrus continued as King of Persia until 530 B.C. when, it is believed, he was killed in battle by the Scythians. It was Cyrus who made the proclamation allowing the Jews to return to Jerusalem to rebuild the temple (2 Chronicles 36:22 – 23 and Ezra 1:1 – 4).

This chapter concludes the historical section of the Book of Daniel. The remainder of the book will focus on the visions and prophecies God gave to Daniel over the span of his life in captivity.

Review Questions

1) Darius the Mede was appointed the ruling governor over Babylon by _____

_____.

2) True or false – Darius ruled as an absolute dictator over Babylon. _____

_____.

3) Why was Daniel given the position as top administrator over the kingdom? _____

_____

_____.

4) Why did the other governing officials conspire against Daniel? _____

_____.

5) What was the big lie these officials told Darius in order to get their proposed decree issued and so as to trap Daniel? _____

_____.

6) Daniel's _____ in his God got him sentenced to death, but his _____ in his God saved him from the jaws of the lions.

7) Daniel's safe deliverance from the lions' den was a miracle, and as a result, Darius issued a new decree which _____

_____.

Up For Discussion

"Then the presidents and princes sought to find occasion against Daniel
concerning the kingdom."
(Daniel 6:4 KJV)

Think back over your years in the workplace, knowing that some of you have obviously spent more time than others just because of your age. Can you ever recall a time when a person or group of persons became jealous of someone in a higher position than they and sought to destroy that person's credibility and bring them down? Maybe they claimed false accusations against that person, or they discovered some weakness then used that weakness to set them up to fail in front of their superiors. All this was done to a good and loyal employee just so that the other person or group could advance or benefit themselves. Share with the class any experience you may have witnessed, or worst, been the victim of.

Chapter 7

This chapter begins a new section in the Book of Daniel. In the first half of the book, Daniel focused on history. In this chapter, beginning the second half of the book, Daniel focuses on prophecy, some of which has already been fulfilled. The main subject of this chapter is Daniel's dream and vision of four beasts. In Nebuchadnezzar's dream of chapter 2, the four world kingdoms were represented by a huge statue made of dazzling metals likened to an idol of worship. God used that image to capture the king's attention. However, in Daniel's dream, God used four carnivorous beasts to represent the vicious character and true nature of these four world kingdoms poised through time and ready to devour mankind. Daniel was also a scholar of Jewish history and remembered the covenant God made with David (2 Samuel 7:16), that One from his line would come to reign forever. Thus, Daniel wondered how God would merge all of this into His sovereign plan for mankind.

Daniel's Dream of Four Beasts

7:1: Daniel has given us the time of his dream as "in the first year of Belshazzar." We have already seen the last day of Belshazzar's reign concluding with the fall of Babylon and his death back in chapter 5. This would indicate the events of chapter 7 precede those of chapter 5. Historical accounts suggest that during the third year of the reign of King Nabonidus of Babylon, he entrusted the kingdom to his oldest son, Belshazzar, while he journeyed away with his army and invaded Arabia. During that time, Nabonidus captured Tema, rebuilt that city, and made it his residence for ten years. Therefore, this would put the dream and visions given to Daniel about fourteen years before the Medes and Persians conquered Babylon – around 553 B.C.

Daniel "wrote down the substance of his dream." As I mentioned back in chapter 5, Daniel may have been moved into a less prominent position of service after the death of Nebuchadnezzar or maybe into retirement. Regardless, he apparently had time and opportunity to study the Word of God and to do some writing. It may have been during this time that he wrote the first part of the Book of Daniel.

7:2: The "four winds of heaven" refers to winds from the north, south, east, and west – from all directions – and "churning up the great sea." In Scripture, the "great sea" refers to the Mediterranean Sea, as it was used to describe the western most boundary of the land allocated to the tribes of Israel (Joshua 15:12 and 23:4). The sea is also symbolic of the nations of the world (Isaiah 17:12). This suggests a storm of great proportion preparing to come upon the world. This storm represents the unsettled and troubled condition of the world from which four great military empires, from nations surrounding the Mediterranean Sea, would subsequently arise to world domination.

7:3: These "four great beasts" represent four great Gentile kingdoms. Each kingdom will be "different from the others" indicates they will be formed out of the many diverse peoples, languages, and nations of the known world, distinct in their geographic origin and ethnicity.

7:4: The lion with the eagle's wings symbolizes Nebuchadnezzar and his Babylonian Empire. He was the head of pure gold from chapter 2. The head of gold represented the outward glory where the lion of this chapter represents the character and cruel nature of this pagan king and his kingdom as we saw in chapters 2 and 3. The lion is often considered the king of beasts, and the eagle is the king of the fowl of the air. Therefore, it is fitting that these two creatures together combine to represent Nebuchadnezzar and his kingdom. When interpreting the king's dream in chapter 2, recall that Daniel referred to Nebuchadnezzar as the "king of kings" (2:37).

The lion's wings "were torn off" likely refers to the humbling of Nebuchadnezzar in his seven-year state of insanity, at which time he ate grass and lived amongst the wild animals (chapter 4). "Stood on two feet" refers to the restoration of his sanity and position as king. Finally, it was given the "heart of a man" refers to Nebuchadnezzar's subsequent acknowledgement and conversion to the one, true living God – the Most High God.

7:5: The bear symbolizes the Media-Persian Empire. In keeping with our image comparison from chapter 2, the bear corresponds with the arms and chest of silver. The fact that it was "raised up on one of its sides" refers to the superior strength and authority of the Persians over the Medes in their alliance. The "three ribs in its mouth" represent the three kingdoms the Medes and Persians devoured, that is, conquered – they were Babylon, Lydia, and Egypt. This westward expansion of the empire into Lydia and Egypt by this enormous and ferocious bear is illustrated here by the words "Get up and eat your fill of flesh!" It was King Xerxes of Persia who continued in this aspiration for expansion by leading his massive army against Greece. However, he suffered a devastating defeat at the hands of the Greeks, who destroyed his navy and drove his armies from their lands.

7:6: The leopard, corresponding with the belly and thighs of bronze of chapter 2, symbolizes the Greece-Macedonian Empire of Alexander the Great. This leopard had "four wings" on its back which would suggest speed or rapidity of movement, and here refers to Alexander's ability to move his armies in order to strike and conquer his adversary with an unanticipated velocity. He launched his attack against the Persians in 334 B.C. and within three years conquered most of the territories through Asia Minor to Egypt; and by 324 B.C., the territories east to the borders of India.

The "four heads" correspond to the four main divisions into which Alexander's empire fell after his untimely death at the age of thirty-three in 323 B.C. The following four generals divided Alexander's empire; each knowing they could not control the entire empire alone:

1) Macedonia and Greece – Cassander
2) Thrace and Asia Minor – Lysimachus
3) Syria and the eastern part of the empire – Seleucus I
4) Palestine, Egypt, and North Africa – Ptolemy I

The Greece-Macedonian Empire falls chronologically between the Old and New Testaments – a period referred to as the Intertestament Period. The Scriptures give us little historical accounting of this empire and its period; however, secular history recorded that during this time the Jewish remnant in Palestine endured a great deal of suffering. Palestine thus became a land bridge and battleground for two emerging empires, the Seleucids of Greece and Western Asia, and the Ptolemies of North Africa. We will study this period in added detail when we look at Daniel's final vision in chapter 11.

7:7: The fourth beast, corresponding with the legs of iron of chapter 2, symbolizes the Roman Empire. More attention is given here to this fourth beast than the other three combined. This beast, Rome, is described as "terrifying and frightening and very powerful" and having "large iron teeth," all characteristic of a vast empire of irresistible strength unmatched by all others that came before. Rome's unrivalled military might "crushed and devoured its victims," and the phrase "trampled underfoot" illustrates the harsh imposition of Rome's culture and laws upon those they conquered. Rome's ability to incite tremendous dread and terror onto the world is no wonder that Daniel's vision of this beast bore no resemblance to any that preceded it.

This beast has "ten horns" which corresponds with the ten toes of the image in chapter 2 and represents the final form of Gentile rule in the end times. For that reason, Daniel's focus was not on the origin of that empire, but rather on the end time, that is, the period of the ten horns. The vision of this fourth beast is important to us today because, unlike the other three beasts [kingdoms], it is thus far unfulfilled. The fourth Gentile kingdom, the Roman Empire, had already appeared; however, over time it disintegrated into semi-barbarian states and lives on today in the many nations of Europe and those bordering the Mediterranean Sea. This empire will be revised one day into its final form during a future time of distress and global chaos.

7:8: Daniel focused next on the ten horns. In Scripture, horns denote a power or authority. These ten horns thus represent ten kingdoms. They do not represent a fifth kingdom because they grow out of the fourth beast and together become the final development of the fourth beast. The toes of the image of chapter 2 were a composite of iron and clay. The iron, Rome, is still there and represents the dictatorial rule of one man. The clay is the weakness and represents the masses of the different nations.

"Another horn, a little one" grew up from among the ten, indicating another powerful ruler. He becomes Daniel's main focus and key to the entire vision. As he grows in power, he "uproots," that is, he destroys three of the ten horns and asserts himself over all. He has "eyes like the eyes of a man," meaning he possesses an astute or highly advanced intelligence. He also has a "mouth that spoke boastfully," denoting the blasphemy of this man. The little horn here and the "beast out of the sea" of Revelation chapter 13 are one and the same. He is the end-time ruler of the revised Roman Empire and the man the Apostle John calls the Antichrist.

Vision of Heaven

7:9 – 10: Daniel's vision now shifts to a scene in heaven and to the throne of God. This is the same vision described by the Apostle John in chapters 4 and 5 of the Book of Revelation. This scene gives us a rare glimpse into heaven, and here it describes the preparation for the impending judgment of the Tribulation Period and the second coming of Christ to earth.

The phrase "thrones were set in place" corresponds with that of Revelation 4:4. In Revelation, John gives us specific details regarding the church; however, Daniel was not concerned with such since the subject of his vision did not include the church.

The "Ancient of Days" is the eternal God and here refers to God the Father. "His clothing was as white as snow" refers to His characteristics of holiness and righteousness. In addition, "the hair of his head was white like wool" speaks of His infinite wisdom – His omniscience.

"His throne was flaming with fire" parallels Revelation 4:5 and denotes His coming judgment. The wheels on His throne were "all ablaze" would suggest a chariot in which God rides to assert His sovereignty and symbolizes the omnipresence of God (Ezekiel 10).

"Fire" speaks of judgment. This verse continues our preview of the preparation for the judgment of the Tribulation Period, referred to by our Lord Jesus Christ as the Great Tribulation. It will conclude with His return to earth to establish His Millennial Kingdom and eternal reign.

"Ten thousand times ten thousand stood before him." These words parallel almost verbatim the words of the Apostle John found in Revelation 5:11: "Then I looked and heard the voice of many angels, numbering thousands upon thousands, and ten thousand times ten thousand." These angels or servants stood before the throne as might jurors in a courtroom stand alongside the judge. The "books" refer to the book of life and the book of works, each containing the names and deeds, respectively, of those who will be judged.

Who has the right to establish justice and righteousness and bring judgment? The words of Jesus in John 5:22 tells us, "Moreover, the Father judges no one, but has entrusted all judgment to the Son."

7:11 – 12: Daniel then switched his attention back to the "horn" – the little horn of verse 8 that grew out of the ten and whose mouth "spoke boastfully." At the same time that God is preparing for the judgment concluding the Great Tribulation, this earthly king is blaspheming the loudest. Again, we see a parallel of this vision by the Apostle John – read Revelation 13:5 – 6. However, the judgment of this brazen king, as described here in Daniel's vision, is his physical death in the fires of hell. In Revelation 19:19 – 21, the Apostle John affirms Daniel's vision and the fate of this ungodly ruler through a similar vision.

It is important for us to keep in mind that the focus with this kingdom in Daniel's vision is not on its beginning, but on its end. The emergence of the "little horn" occurs in our future, during the dreadful Tribulation Period and seven years prior to the return of Christ to earth to judge the nations and those surviving this period of extreme judgment upon the world and mankind.

"The other beasts" might refer to the remaining seven kingdoms that were allowed to live on in a subservient role under the rule of the little horn [Antichrist] after the first three were "uprooted" or destroyed. The time period here would be the Great Tribulation Period. Other scholars contend that this is a reference to the empires of Babylon, Media-Persia, and Greece, the three beasts of verses 4 – 6, since they "had their dominion taken away" (KJV). I believe both explanations are equally justified given the overall context of Daniel's vision.

7:13 – 14: Daniel said he saw "one like a son of man," meaning what he saw was not a man as such, but was rather the perfect manifestation of humanity. The Son of Man is the Messiah – Jesus Christ.

Jesus applied this name phrase to Himself to emphasize His humanity as the incarnate Son of God (Matthew 8:20). The Apostle John used this same phrase in his description of the glorified Christ found in Revelation 1:13 and 14:14.

"Coming with the clouds of heaven" is an expression used to speak of our Lord Jesus Christ coming in judgment. In Revelation 1:7, the Apostle John wrote, "Look, he is coming with the clouds, and every eye will see him, even those who pierced him; and all the people of the earth will mourn because of him." Likewise, in His Olivet Discourse with His disciples, Jesus told them, "At that time the sign of the Son of Man will appear in the sky, and all the nations of the earth will mourn. They will see the Son of Man coming on the clouds of the sky, with power and great glory" (Matthew 24:30). Even as He stood on trial before the Sanhedrin, our Lord Jesus again referred to this passage when asked if He was the Christ: "I am … And you will see the Son of Man sitting at the right hand of the Mighty One and coming on the clouds of heaven" (Mark 14:62).

These verses pave the way for the coming of Christ and make it abundantly clear that the Lord Jesus is the "Rock" that was "cut out, but not by human hands" and will smash the image and "crush all those kingdoms and bring them to an end, but it will itself endure forever" from chapter 2. Following the final day of the Tribulation Period, the Lord Jesus Christ will return to earth as Warrior and Judge to put down all wickedness and rebellion. The Apostle John describes this scene in detail (Revelation 19:11 – 16). The psalmist likewise proclaimed, "Ask of me, and I will make the nations your inheritance, the ends of the earth your possession. You will rule them with an iron scepter; you will dash them to pieces like pottery" (Psalm 2:8 – 9). The Lord Jesus will establish His kingdom on earth, and His authority and sovereignty will be absolute. Unlike the vanishing nature of the previous empires, His kingdom will be "an everlasting dominion" and "one that will never be destroyed." Read aloud the words of the prophet found in Micah 4:1 – 5.

The Interpretation of Daniel's Dream

7:15 – 16: Recall from chapter 2 how Nebuchadnezzar was troubled by his vision of the image. Likewise, Daniel was also troubled by the king's dream; however, here Daniel was further grieved by his own vision. Daniel "approached one of those standing there," referring to an angel, for an explanation.

7:17: The four beasts represent four kingdoms or kings (KJV). Kings are synonymous with their kingdoms. These great beasts with their ferocious and carnivorous nature represent the character of both the kings and their respective kingdoms.

7:18: The identity of "the saints" is crucial here in our context of Daniel's dream since the term is used again in four subsequent verses of this chapter and referenced yet again in Daniel 8:24. The Greek word for saints is *hagios*, which means "holy" or holy ones. One today might jump to the assumption that these saints are New Testament saints – believers that make up the church. However, there were Old Testament saints too. The people of the nation of Israel were considered saints (Exodus 19:6), along with their Gentile converts. They were saved and set apart for God by their righteousness that came through faith and obedience. There will also be those, both Jew and Gentile, who are saved during the dreadful Tribulation Period (Revelation 13:7), after the church is removed from the earth at the rapture. You see, God has never stopped saving people in every generation, since the beginning of time, and He is not going to stop until His Son Jesus Christ returns to earth to establish His eternal kingdom.

Here in the Book of Daniel, the word "saints" has specific reference, it is to those Old Testament patriarchs and the people of the nation of Israel; but not all of the people – only the believing and obedient remnant. The church saints are not a part of Daniel's visions because the church age was never revealed to Daniel or any other Old Testament prophet.

7:19 – 20: God returned Daniel's focus to the fourth beast. Our focus today should be on this as well since the timing of this beast [empire] likely falls in our imminent future.

These verses speak to us of ferocity and immense strength, and the unrestrained capacity of an empire that conquers and subdues everything in its path. The viciousness of this beast with its "iron teeth" is mentioned here again, along with the addition of its "bronze claws." The empire of Rome was feared and hated by every nation it occupied. Rome rejected the Son of God – the Messiah Jesus Christ. It was a Roman official who ordered His crucifixion. Subsequently, Christians were persecuted mercilessly by the Romans well into the third century A.D.

The ten horns, corresponding to the ten toes of the image in chapter 2, grow out of the fourth beast and represent its final development – not a fifth kingdom. It is thus logical to assume that horns do not grow out of a dead beast. As I mentioned earlier, Rome lives on today, shattered in fragments amongst the many nations of Europe and those bordering the Mediterranean Sea, likely some of Asia as well. Rome will be revised in its ultimate form some day in our future. The identity of the ten nations that emerge to make up this last great empire would be pure speculation on anyone's part. However, during this time, three of those ten will fall to their destruction before the "other horn that came up." The "other horn" is the "little horn" of verse 8, and he will grow into absolute power and appeal to become the final end-time ruler of the world. The Apostle Paul calls him the "man of lawlessness" (2 Thessalonians 2:3). Likewise, the Apostle John calls him the "beast … out of the sea" (Revelation 13:1) and labels him the "Antichrist" (1 John 2:18).

7:21 – 22: The "horn was waging war against the saints." Rome will rise again to be a world power during a future time of turmoil under the tyrannical rule of Antichrist. In Revelation 13:7, the Apostle John's vision parallels that of Daniel's here where he tells us, "He was given power to make war against the saints and to conquer them. And he was given authority over every tribe, people, language and nation." This is a reference to the last half of the Tribulation Period (the church is removed from the earth by our Lord at the rapture prior to the Tribulation Period). Antichrist will emerge onto the world stage during this time of chaos and conquer the hearts of the people through diplomacy, promising peace and prosperity. He will be the one who puts the Roman Empire back together as he rises to power and ultimately becomes ruler of the united world. The "saints" of this passage refer to those who reject the rule of Antichrist and are obedient to God through faith in His Son Jesus Christ during the Tribulation Period (reference 7:18).

Today the world, and Europe specifically, is being prepared for a one-world government philosophy. That philosophy, inspired by Satan and promoted by the atheistic and secular leaders of world governments today, is rapidly spreading across the earth.

The "Ancient of Days" is the eternal God and here refers to the Lord Jesus Christ, for the words of our Lord tell us, "I and the Father are one" (John 10:30). All judgment has been entrusted to the Son, the Lord Jesus Christ. He will return to earth personally at the "pronounced" time, for He is the only One who is able to put down the kingdom and rule of Antichrist.

The "saints," who will possess the kingdom, again are not church age saints – the reference is to those Old Testament saints and the faithful and obedience remnant of the nation of Israel. The church age with its saints was never revealed to Daniel.

7:23 – 25: The fourth beast, as related back in verse 17, is identified again here as a fourth kingdom. The kings (verse 17 of the KJV) are synonymous with their kingdoms. The fourth kingdom represents the Roman Empire along with its succession of dictatorial rulers.

There are "ten horns" that represent "ten kings" that, in turn also represent ten kingdoms. They "come from this [fourth] kingdom" and now represent the final form of the fourth kingdom. The eleventh "king will arise," meaning he will rise in power by destroying three of the other kings. He will ultimately rise to become the dictator of the entire world. The connection between Daniel's "little horn" and John's "beast out of the sea" is without doubt. Recall that John says, "And he was given authority over every tribe, people, language and nation" (Revelation 13:7b). He is the man of lawlessness, the Antichrist, and he is the end-time ruler of the world during the dreadful Tribulation Period.

"He will speak against the Most High," means he speaks blasphemous words against God. The Apostle John tells us that, "He opened his mouth to blaspheme God, and to slander his name and his dwelling place and those who live in heaven" (Revelation 13:6). One of the characteristics of Antichrist is that he is against God and against Christ. The Apostle Paul, when writing about the man of lawlessness says that, "He will oppose and exalt himself over everything that is called God or is worshiped, so that he sets himself up in God's temple, proclaiming himself to be God" (2 Thessalonians 2:4). Yet again, in 1 John 2:22 the apostle explains, "Who is the liar? It is the man who denies that Jesus is the Christ. Such a man is the antichrist – he denies the Father and the Son." The second characteristic of Antichrist is that he imitates Christ. We see both characteristics manifested in the two beasts of chapter 13 in the Book of Revelation.

"And oppress his saints" refers to persecution. Just as Rome ruthlessly persecuted the Christians well into the third century following Christ's death, so also will Antichrist relentlessly pursue and persecute anyone whose faith and allegiance is to God and in opposition to him.

The reign of the "little horn" is short-lived, for Daniel said, "the saints will be handed over to him for" the following time period:

1) "Time" refers to one year.
2) "Times" refers to two years.
3) "Half a time" refers to one half of a year.

The sum total is three and a half years. Antichrist will reign over the world during the last three and a half years of the seven-year Tribulation Period. The same period of time is confirmed in the Apostle John's vision of the beast. He says that the beast will "exercise his authority for forty-two months" (Revelation 13:5). In response to His disciple's questions concerning the end of the age, it is no wonder that our Lord Jesus spoke so bluntly of this time of great distress: "If those days had not been cut short, no one would survive, but for the sake of the elect [the saints] those days will be shortened" (Matthew 24:22).

7:26: "The court will sit." This verse brings us back to the scene in heaven we saw back in verses 9 – 10. God the Father is on the central throne and His Son Jesus Christ is the executor of judgment against the beast. This king and his global empire must be "completely destroyed forever." The judgment continues through and to the end of the Tribulation Period and is concluded by the return of Christ to earth to establish His eternal kingdom. Christ's return ends the "time of the Gentiles" that began with Nebuchadnezzar well over two millenniums ago.

7:27: "His kingdom will be an everlasting kingdom" is a reference to Christ's eternal kingdom on earth that begins with His Millennial reign (Revelation 20). The Millennium, described by the prophet in Isaiah 65:17 – 25, is merely a thousand-year period of testing of mankind, and then it continues on into eternity.

7:28: Daniel said that he was "deeply troubled," and that he kept the matter to himself. Daniel chose not to share these visions with his colleagues because he knew they concerned the future and its end times. The dream and its visions troubled him to the point that it changed his overall view of things concerning his faith in God, as well it should. The prayerful study of prophecy should have a humbling and transforming effect upon the life of any believer.

Review Questions

1) Daniel's dream of four beasts corresponds with Nebuchadnezzar's dream of an enormous dazzling statue of metal. Though each dream represents four kingdoms, the beasts of Daniel's dream are representative of what? _____

_____.

2) In Scripture, the "great sea" refers to _____.

3) The bear in Daniel's dream symbolizes the Media-Persian Empire, and the "three ribs in its mouth" refer to _____.

4) The leopard in Daniel's dream symbolizes the Greece-Macedonian Empire of Alexander the Great, and the "four heads" represent _____

_____.

5) The "terrifying and frightening" fourth beast in Daniel's dream represents the Roman Empire, and the "ten horns" represent _____.

6) The "little horn" that rises in power from among the ten horns and destroys three represents

_____.

7) His reign will end with his destruction when _____

_____.

Up for Discussion

"It was diverse from all the beasts that were before it; and it had ten horns."
(Daniel 7:7 KJV)

How much do you follow current events in the world? Discuss events that may appear as though the world, including the United States, is moving closer to a one-world order. One example might be our nation's massive debt resulting in the eventual devaluation of the US dollar and the call for a global currency. In 1999, the euro was introduced and is today the single currency shared by 18 of the European Union's Member States, which together make up the euro area.

Another example might be the continued growth in the size of government and the freedoms we compromise for the good of the greater population.

Keep in mind this is an area of great debate, so be sensitive and tolerant of the opinions of others in the class.

Chapter 8

The subject of this chapter is Daniel's vision of the ram and the goat, and its subsequent interpretation. This vision was prophetic when Daniel recorded it; however, the events of the vision have since been literally and undeniably fulfilled. It is for this reason that liberal critics today dispute the supernatural ability to predict long-range future and deny the sixth century B.C. authorship of Daniel, as I mentioned in the book's introduction.

Daniel's vision here of the ram with two unequaled horns and the goat places greater focus on the conflict between the second and third world empires – the Media-Persian and the Greece-Macedonian empires. This vision includes "another horn," similar to the "little horn" we have previously seen. However, this "horn" grows out of the third kingdom (not the fourth), and has already been fulfilled in Antiochus IV Epiphanes. His persecution of the Jews became so horrific that it earned him the nick-name Epimanes, "the madman" of Jewish history.

Additionally, beginning in this chapter, Daniel reverted back to writing in Hebrew and continued through the remainder of the book in that language. Recall that in our previous section (Daniel 2:4 – 7:28), Daniel switched to writing in Aramaic because he was speaking in the language of the world concerning matters of importance to the Gentile nations of the time. The subject matter, going forward, will focus on special concerns of God's chosen people – the nation of Israel – therefore, Daniel switched his emphasis and writing back to Hebrew.

Daniel's Vision of a Ram and a Goat

8:1: As in chapter 7, Daniel gives us the time of his vision, this one occurring in the "third year" of the reign of King Belshazzar, about 551 B.C. Therefore, both the visions of chapter 7 and the vision given here to Daniel take place before the end of the Babylonian empire and precede the events of chapter 5.

8:2: The setting of Daniel's vision is important to us – it was not Babylon. Though Daniel was physically in Babylon at the time, in his dream he envisioned himself in the "citadel of Susa" or "palace of Shushan" (KJV), which was the capital of the Media-Persian Empire – the second world empire. Susa was located about 230 miles east of Babylon. The "Ulai Canal" was an artificial irrigation canal located near Susa. The vision given to Daniel as he sat on the banks of the River Ulai concerned the second and third world empires.

8:3 – 4: The "ram with two horns" represents the Media-Persian Empire (verse 20) and foresees the two-nation alliance that replaces Babylon.

The first horn represents the Medes, under general Gobryas, with their siege and overthrow of Babylon. The longer horn "grew up later" represents the Persian monarchs that later gained supremacy over the Medes under Cyrus the Great and took the combined empire to its ultimate heights.

This is the empire that was represented by the bear in chapter 7 and the arms and chest of silver in chapter 2 (see end of chapter illustration: The Four Gentile Kingdoms – Chapter Comparison). Media-Persia with its eastern-most edge bordering India "charged" west and conquered Babylon, Syria, and Asia Minor. It charged north and conquered Armenia and the Caspian Sea region. Lastly, it charged south and conquered Egypt and Ethiopia.

8:5 – 7: The "goat" is Greece (verse 21) and its "prominent horn" represents Alexander the Great. As the Persian army pressed western toward Europe, this goat from the west charged across the "whole earth without touching the ground." This phrase corresponds with the leopard with four wings on its back (7:6), and is representative here of the speed with which Alexander and his armies moved in conquering their adversaries. He launched his attack against the Persians in 334 B.C. and within three years conquered most of the territories through Asia Minor to Egypt and east to the borders of India. Alexander's conquest was so rapid that it seemed as if he flew across the earth.

Paving the way for Alexander's "charge" was an alliance of Greek city-states and their earlier victories over the invading forces of Media-Persia, under King Xerxes, in the battles of Salamis and Plataea. Though the Persian forces outnumbered the Greeks, the Greek soldier, in his own right, was a far better trained and disciplined opponent to come against. The Persian army and navy were decisively defeated as Xerxes retreated to Asia. These two battles marked the turning point in the Greco-Persian wars, and from then on, the Greeks took over the offensive.

Alexander the Great rose as ruler of the Greek kingdom of Macedonia to succeed his father, Philip II at the age of twenty. He was a young general and military genius who spent most of his ruling years on an unprecedented military campaign through Asia and northeast Africa. About the same time, Darius III came to the throne in Persia. In a series of decisive battles, most notably the battles of Issus and battle of Gaugamela, Alexander and his forces "trampled," meaning he overthrew Darius III and thus ended the Persian Empire in 331 B.C. Later, by the age of thirty-two, Alexander the Great had created one of the largest empires of the ancient world.

8:8: "His large horn was broken off" refers to Alexander's untimely death at the age of thirty-three and at the height of his career. He died in Babylon of fever after attending a party where, many historians believe, he was poisoned.

The "four prominent horns" that grew up correspond to the four smaller kingdoms into which Alexander's empire fell after his death in 323 B.C. The "four winds of heaven" refer to the four directions from which the wind blows. The following four generals divided Alexander's empire – each knowing they were not powerful enough to control the entire empire alone:

1) West – Macedonia and Greece – Cassander
2) North – Thrace and Asia Minor – Lysimachus

3) East – Syria and the eastern part of the empire – Seleucus I
4) South – Palestine, Egypt, and North Africa – Ptolemy I

8:9 – 10: The "Beautiful Land" is Israel. The "small horn" or "little horn" (KJV) here that "grew in power" is not the same as the "little horn" described in chapter 7. The little horn of chapter 7 grew out of the fourth kingdom, Rome, whereas the little horn here grows out of the third kingdom, Greece. The "little horn" here refers to Antiochus IV Epiphanes, who came out of Syria from the Seleucid Empire to rule from 175 B.C. to 164 B.C.

Antiochus Epiphanes became a type of Antichrist because of his aggressive anti-Semitic actions that resulted in the slaughter of thousands of Jews. He also desecrated the temple in Jerusalem by erecting a statue of Zeus in the Holy Place and dedicated the temple to the Olympian god. He also sacrificed swine on the Altar of Burned Offerings. This was the first "abomination of desolation." He became known as Epimanes – "the madman."

The "host of the heavens" and the "starry host" refer to God's people (12:3). The "trampling" of these godly believers drastically illustrates the brutal persecution of the Jewish people, and their faith, during the reign of Antiochus.

8:11 – 12: The "Prince of host" is the eternal God. In 168 B.C., the little horn, Antiochus Epiphanes, attacked and captured Jerusalem and executed countless Jews. During this time, he plundered the temple and exalted himself claiming to be equal to God. Antiochus also outlawed all Jewish religious rites and traditions and desecrated the temple as I described above. In Isaiah 12:12 – 14, the prophet described how Lucifer had the same aspiration to be like God.

Let's keep in mind that God is sovereign – He exalts and deposes all rulers – and it was only by His permissive will that this little horn "prospered" during this dreadful time of Jewish history.

8:13: The "holy ones" or "saints" (KJV) conversing here are angels. We described angels earlier (4:13) as a heavenly order of created beings who administer the will of God in the world and His universe. The desecration of the temple explained above is referred to here as "the rebellion that causes desolation."

8:14: "2,300 evenings and mornings." There is a bit of disagreement amongst scholars as to the interpretation of this numbered phrase. I lean toward the view that since there was two daily sacrifices required for Israel's atonement (Exodus 29:38 – 42), then the "2,300 evenings and mornings" refer to the number of consecutive sacrifices offered on 1,150 days.

This would closely correspond with the time interval between the pollution of the temple by Antiochus in 168 B.C. and the cleansing and rededication of the temple by the Jewish priest, Judas Maccabeus in December 165 B.C. The army of Judas Maccabeus drove out the Syrian army of the Seleucid Empire and recaptured Jerusalem in what historians refer to as the Maccabean Revolt. Their victory resulted in the establishment of an independent Jewish state and the Hasmonean kingdom. The rededication of the temple is commemorated today as the Festival of Hanukkah. It is also known as the Festival of Lights and the Feast of Dedication. This was one of the holy festivals celebrated at the time of Christ (John 10:22). It was not mentioned in the Old Testament because it was established in the Intertestament Period – the time between the Old and New Testaments.

The Meaning of the Vision

8:15 – 16: While Daniel was pondering the vision, the angel Gabriel appeared to him. This is the first mention of the messenger Gabriel in Scripture.

8:17 – 18: "Son of man" is a term used 93 times in the Book of Ezekiel (starting in 2:1) to emphasize the prophet's humanity when being addressed by a holy presence – here being the angel Gabriel.

Gabriel's explanation in these remaining verses make it abundantly clear that Antiochus IV Epiphanes is merely a foreshadowing of the coming of the end-time Antichrist. "The time of the end" places the complete fulfillment of this prophecy during the seven-year Tribulation Period, a period our Lord Jesus called the Great Tribulation (Matthew 24:21 KJV). The prophecy goes beyond Daniel's immediate future and looks forward into the distant future – a future that yet today remains unfulfilled. Antiochus was but a prototype of the other "little horn," the Antichrist, who would come at the end of the "times of the Gentiles" (1 John 2:18).

8:19: Gabriel again moves the vision from its imminent fulfillment in Antiochus to a "later" or future "time of wrath" – a reference to the Great Tribulation Period. The "appointed time of the end" corresponds with the end of the "times of the Gentiles" (Luke 21:24), and culminates with Christ's return to earth to put an end to all rebellion and unrighteousness and to establish His eternal kingdom.

8:20 – 22: In the meantime, Gabriel clearly identifies the ram as the "two-horned" alliance of the nations of Media and Persia. Likewise, the goat represents the "king [kingdom] of Greece," and its "large horn," its first king – Alexander the Great. Lastly, Gabriel identifies the "four horns that replaced the one that was broken off" as the four smaller kingdoms into which Alexander's empire would fall after his ill-timed death; and not one of the four would rule with the same "power" and strength as did Alexander.

8:23 – 24: "In the latter part of their reign, when rebels have become completely wicked" is a reference to the time of the end when the sinful actions of mankind reach the point where God can no longer tolerate them without bringing judgment (Matthew 23:32, 1 Thessalonians 2:14 – 16). Although these verses look ahead to the rise of the end-time Antichrist (the "little horn of chapter 7), they also illustrate the parallel of the rise of the other "little horn" of this chapter. The other "little horn," that grew out of the third kingdom, is Antiochus IV Epiphanes of the Seleucid Empire of Syria. His rise as "king" after the assassination of Seleucus was accomplished through deceit and "intrigue" since he was not the rightful successor to the Seleucid throne.

His strength was "not by his own power" indicates that Antiochus was Satan incarnate and possessed supernatural wisdom and powers only possible through the work of Satan in him, as will also be the case with the end-time Antichrist. The Apostle Paul called Antichrist the "man of lawlessness" and wrote, "The coming of the lawless one will be in accordance with the work of Satan …" (2 Thessalonians 2:9). The Apostle John referred to him as the beast: "The dragon [Satan] gave the beast [Antichrist] his power and his throne and great authority" (Revelation 13:2b).

"He will destroy the mighty men" demonstrates the extent to which these depraved men will murder and depose in order to firmly establish their autocratic position. Antiochus murdered a second legitimate heir to secure his throne, and Daniel revealed earlier that Antichrist would overthrow and destroy three kings (and kingdoms) to consummate his dictatorship (7:24).

The "holy people" refers to the Jews – the nation of Israel. The slaughter of countless Jews by Antiochus was horrific – as bad as Hitler's campaign. However, his actions were just a foreshadowing of the Antichrist who is coming at the time of the end. The Apostle John tells us, "The dragon [Satan indwelled Antichrist] was enraged at the woman [Israel] and went off to make war against the rest of her offspring" (Revelation 12:17). Both men are pawns of Satan. Satan's purpose has always been to get nations warring against each other, and his energy has always been directed at the nation of Israel. Satan initiated what Bible scholars refer to as "the conflict of the ages," with Satan attempting to stamp out the seed of the woman [Israel] from the time of Adam (Genesis 3:15) to the time of the end. The prophecy contained here in Daniel's vision, thus has great consequence for the nation of Israel, and that was why Daniel switched his writing back to the Hebrew as I mentioned earlier in our chapter introduction.

8:25: Antiochus Epiphanes was merely a "type" (short for prototype) of the king who is coming at the time of the end – Antichrist. The end-time Antichrist will do, on a much greater scale, four things that Antiochus, by contrast, did in miniature:

1) "He will cause deceit to prosper." The Lord Jesus made reference to Antichrist with His warning: "For false Christs and false prophets will appear and perform great signs and miracles to deceive even the elect – if that were possible" (Matthew 24:24).
2) "He will consider himself superior." The Apostle John said that Antichrist was "given to utter proud words and blasphemies and to exercise his authority for forty-two months" (Revelation 13:5). Antichrist will be Satan indwelled, and like Satan, he will be filled with egotistical pride.
3) "When they feel secure, he will destroy many." During the first half of the Tribulation Period, Antichrist will rise to power through diplomacy, ushering in a false peace and presenting himself as a global problem solver. However, the peace that he brings is temporary. At the mid-point of the Tribulation, Antichrist will set himself up as dictator of the world, for the Apostle John tells us, "He was given power to make war against the saints and to conquer them. And he was given authority over every tribe, people, language and nation" (Revelation 13:7). At that time, he will also demand universal worship of himself and of his image, and those who refuse will be "killed" (Revelation 13:15). This is reminiscent of Nebuchadnezzar and his image of chapter 3.
4) He will "take his stand against the Prince of princes." The Prince of princes is Jesus Christ. Antichrist will oppose and fight against Christ. The Apostle John writes: "Then I saw the beast [Antichrist] and the kings of the earth and their armies gather to make war against the rider on the horse [Christ] and his army" (Revelation 19:19). One of the two characteristics of Antichrist is that he is against Christ (1 John 2:22). The second characteristic of Antichrist is that he imitates Christ (Revelation 13:3).

He "will be destroyed, but not by human hands" is the fate of both – Antiochus and Antichrist. According to the apocryphal Book of 1 Maccabees, Antiochus died suddenly while in Persia of a painful disease; thus, God "destroyed" him. Likewise, the end-time Antichrist will be destroyed by the Son of God, Jesus Christ, upon His return to earth to establish His righteous and eternal kingdom. The Apostle Paul explained, "And then the lawless one will be revealed, whom the Lord

Jesus will overthrow with the breath of his mouth and destroy by the splendor of his coming" (2 Thessalonians 2:8).

8:26: Daniel's writings, as well as other documents of the time were written on scrolls which could be rolled up and sealed in clay jars to protect them. Daniel was told that his vision was "true," but concerned the "distant future," and thus should be sealed and stored away for a later time.

8:27: Daniel was greatly "appalled" by this vision just as he was with his visions in chapter 7. The fact that God was merging the "time of the Gentiles" with the history of the nation of Israel was becoming quite puzzling to Daniel, to the extent that he said it was "beyond understanding."

For us today, we make up yet another component of God's plan for mankind which Daniel never foresaw, and that is the "church." The word church comes from the Greek word meaning the "called out ones." Christians are the "called out ones" – the people of faith in God's plan of salvation through His Son Jesus Christ. Once we are removed from this earth at the rapture, God will again turn His attention to and complete His purpose for the nation of Israel and the time of the Gentiles.

Review Questions

1) Daniel was physically in Babylon, but in his dream, he envisioned himself where? _____
   _____.

2) The ram in Daniel's vision represented the empire of Media-Persia and its longer horn represented what? _____

3) The goat in Daniel's vision represented the empire of Greece-Macedonia and its prominent horn represented what? _____.

4) What was meant by the large horn breaking off and in its place four others grew? _____
   _____.

5) Another horn grew out of one of the four. What did this horn represent? _____
   _____.

6) The angel Gabriel revealed the dream to Daniel, and then switched the focus to the distant future – why? _____
   _____.

7) Why was Daniel appalled by the vision? _____
   _____.

Up For Discussion

We have seen in chapter 5 how easily the kingdom of Babylon was captured and overthrown on the night that its residing ruler, King Belshazzar, was holding an elaborate party for his nobles. There was much drinking of wine that night; and while under the influence of alcohol, the king ordered the sacred goblets taken from the temple in Jerusalem brought in so they could drink from them as well. As a consequence, God brought judgment down upon the king and his kingdom that very night.

Historians tell us that Alexander the Great likely suffered from alcoholism. His drinking bouts evidently were legendary. It was said that he once killed a friend, who had saved his life in battle, with a spear. He wept remorsefully for three days following. Alexander became increasing unpredictable and paranoid. Finally, it is believed that at a private party (in Babylon no less), Alexander drank a huge quantity of wine and hours later died.

Apparently, two great empires – Babylon and Greece – fell in a drunken orgy. The common denominator was alcohol. Look at Washington today. Many decisions and policies are made during after-hours cocktail parties. We watch as the legalization of marijuana becomes increasingly more accepted, all the while ignoring the growing national statistics attributed to the crippling use of these and other intoxicants.

Does Scripture and its history teach us anything as a nation? Is America destined to fall because of its indulgence? Will God judge us similarly?

The Four Gentile Kingdoms – Chapter Comparison

Chapter 2	Chapter 7	Chapter 8	Empire Chronology
Head of Pure Gold	Lion		Babylonian Empire 626 B.C.-539 B.C.
Chest and Arms of Silver	Bear	Ram	Media-Persian Empire 539 B.C.-331 B.C.
Belly and Thighs of Bronze	Leopard	Goat	Greece-Macedonian Empire 330 B.C.-146 B.C.
Legs Of Iron	Terrifying and Frightening Beast		Roman Empire 63 B.C. through the Fall of Jerusalem in 70 A.D.
Feet of Iron and Clay			Revised Roman Empire "The Latter Days"

Chapter 9

This is one of the most incredible chapters in all of Scripture because of its extraordinary dual subject matter – prayer and prophecy – each, in their own right, being amongst the greatest in nature and example to be found in the Word of God. In verses 3 – 21, we have the prayer of Daniel with its basic elements that together form the foundation on which other prayers in the Bible are modeled (for example, Nehemiah 1:4 – 11). As we will see, Daniel's prayer gets an immediate response. The remaining six verses give us the very important prophecy of the Seventy "Sevens" or "Weeks" (KJV).

9:1: Daniel chronicled the year of these events as during the "first year of Darius … the Mede." Therefore, we are picking up where we left off at the end of chapter 5, after the fall of Babylon and the appointment of Darius as "ruler over the Babylonian kingdom" by Cyrus the Great of Persia, 539 – 538 B.C. This time period closely corresponds with that of chapter 6.

9:2: Recall that during the reign of Belshazzar, king of Babylon, Daniel recorded his dreams and the visions they contained which he described as "troubling" (chapter 7) and "appalling" (chapter 8). Both dreams concerned the Gentile world empires and their rule over his people, the nation of Israel. Next, Daniel witnessed the fall of Babylon and the rise of a new world empire – Persia. Daniel was perplexed and began to wonder about the future and his people; too, he was likely disturbed by the vision of the little horn [Antiochus – chapter 8] who would persecute his people and desecrate the temple. Consequently, Daniel turned to a study of the Word of God, here referred to as the "Scriptures." He read the book of the Prophet Jeremiah who predicted the following concerning Israel: "This whole country will become a desolate wasteland, and these nations will serve the king of Babylon seventy years" (Jeremiah 25:11); and, "This is what the Lord says: 'When seventy years are completed for Babylon, I will come to you and fulfill my gracious promise to bring you back to this place'" (Jeremiah 29:10).

Daniel was in his mid-teens and among the first group of captives deported to Babylon about 605 B.C. He had grown to be an old man in his eighties, and thus he realized the period of captivity for his people was nearly complete, and soon his people would be given an opportunity to return to their home land. The fact that Daniel "understood" this "from the Scriptures" points out the importance of studying the Word of God. This was what brought Daniel to prayer. The Word reveals the will of God. A study of God's Word, followed by prayer, is the most comprehensive way for determining God's will.

Daniel's Prayer

Based on the promises he found in the Book of Jeremiah, Daniel's prayer revealed his life-long character as a man of prayer. From the early years of his exile and service to King Nebuchadnezzar of Babylon to the time of his new king, Darius, Daniel never compromised his faith in God or discipline in his prayer life. Daniel was a man of prayer, and his prayer introduces us to those basic elements that are the essence of genuine prayer:

1) Prayer should begin with purposeful *praise* and *worship*. Daniel said he "pleaded with him [God] in prayer." Daniel praised God as "great and awesome." Prayer should not be a repetition of idle requests or the forming together of poetic phrases. Our Lord Jesus told the crowd, "And when you pray, do not keep on babbling like pagans, for they think they will be heard because of their many words" (Matthew 6:7).

2) Prayer, as with our discipleship, should demonstrate *humility* and *sacrifice*. Daniel fasted, and prayed in sackcloth, not for an outwardly show, but to demonstrate his humility and sincere heart. Most of us today live a life of plenty, thus I am sure there are many worldly things we can put aside or do without in order to make our prayer lives more meaningful and sincere. For instance, set a specific time each day to spend in disciplined prayer.

3) Prayer should include *confession*. You cannot ignore or hide your sin from God, so don't beat around the bush about it.

4) Prayer *petition* should be firmly grounded in faith so that God's glory and perfect will becomes the priority and purpose of your request. Daniel's petition was so strong that he got an immediate answer from God. Daniel got answers to all his prayers. The Apostle John told believers that they have this same power through faith in the Son of God – Jesus Christ: "This is the confidence we have in approaching God: that if we ask anything according to his will, he hears us" (1 John 5:14). This is true for us today!

Though Daniel's prayer is considered one of the longest prayers in the Old Testament, it really takes only three or four minutes when you read it start to finish. One last thing I would like to mention is that Daniel prayed privately. Our Lord Jesus often prayed privately as well (John 17). We do not always have to call a prayer meeting in times of distress, every one of us can be a mighty prayer warrior on our own if we simply follow Daniel's example.

9:3 – 4: Daniel "turned to the Lord God … in fasting." The gospels tell us that our Lord Jesus fasted "forty days and forty nights" (Matthew 4:2; Luke 4:2). However, today fasting is not a required service for the people of God. It is merely something one could do over and above their usual prayer practice. In the early years of the church, there were many who fasted, including the Apostle Paul (2 Corinthians 11:27). The point is that Daniel used fasting to purposefully demonstrate humility and sacrifice in his worship to God.

Daniel's prayer was personal because it concerned himself and his people. He went to his knees and with his face to the ground; and the first words he expressed were in praise: "O Lord, the great and awesome God." Before making any confession or petition, Daniel focused on the greatness of God. Next, Daniel acknowledged that God "keeps his covenant of love," meaning His promises. God makes promises and God keeps His promises. God is faithful. The KJV uses the word "mercy." It was because of His love and mercy that Daniel and his people were allowed to live and prosper while captive in Babylon. It is by that same love and mercy that He saves us today. The Prophet

Jeremiah wrote, "Because of the Lord's great love we are not consumed, for his compassions never fail" (Lamentations 3:22). God is gracious, but God expects us to obey Him.

9:5 – 6: Daniel used the pronoun "we," and thus identified himself with his people long ago when they were living in the Promised Land and chose to rebel against God. This is a prayer of repentance for Israel's sinful past. It reached all the way back to King Solomon when, in his older years, he turned his back on God by taking wives from the pagan nations around him and following their gods (1 Kings 11:4 – 8). Daniel was quite specific in his confession and left nothing out. He recorded each sin: wickedness, rebellion, disobedience, and refusal to listen and follow God's prophets. Our confession should be likewise. It is not enough to say, "I have sinned." Like Daniel, we need to be specific about our sins to God. We should lay it all out there in front of Him, regardless of how ugly or cruel it may seem to us – God already knows all of it. You cannot hide your sin from God, so just be open and honest with Him.

9:7 – 14: Daniel continued his confession to God in these verses. Daniel acknowledged that as a result of their "unfaithfulness," God had "shamed" the people of Israel and "scattered" them amongst the surrounding nations. Some lived as captives along with Daniel in Babylon while others were dispersed to nations "near and far."

Daniel's confession illustrated God's goodness – His mercy and forgiveness, in contrast to Israel's sin – their rebellion and disobedience. It also demonstrated God righteousness in contrast to Israel's shame. Israel was scattered because of their disobedience to God in violation of His covenant. God had given the land to Israel as an unconditional covenant – a permanent covenant. However, Israel's occupation in the land was based on their obedience to God's law given in the Law of Moses – that was a conditional covenant. Obedience would result in rewards and disobedience in curses and punishment (Leviticus 26; Deuteronomy 28, 29), and the most devastating curse would be banishment for the people of Israel from their Promised Land (Leviticus 26:33 – 39; Deuteronomy 4:27; 28:36 – 37, 63 – 68). Lastly, Daniel's confession proved that God was right, the curse had come to pass, and that he and his people got exactly the punishment they deserved.

God is always right – that is, righteous in what He does. We cannot go to God and make excuses for our sin, that would be like saying God made a mistake. God does not make mistakes; we are the ones who are wrong, and we need to go to Him in true and humble confession. Only then can we fall upon and claim the mercy of God. Daniel understood this and his prayer illustrated it.

9:15 – 18: Daniel began his petition by first reflecting back on Israel's greatest deliverance, the exodus of "your people out of Egypt." God redeemed Israel out of Egypt because of His righteousness, not because of theirs. The Scriptures tell us, "God heard their groaning and he remembered his covenant with Abraham, with Isaac, and with Jacob. So God looked on the Israelites and was concerned about them" (Exodus 2:24 – 25). God redeemed Israel from Egypt because He saw their misery and remembered His mercy.

"O Lord, in keeping with all your righteous acts" was Daniel's petition. Part of adopting an attitude of humility in prayer is acknowledging that God's justice demands the punishment of sin. Jerusalem had become a desolate wasteland, the temple laid in ruin, and the Jewish people had become "an object of scorn to all." Daniel asked that God would repeat Himself and deliver His people again from their captivity as He did so long ago. Daniel asked this because of God's righteousness – "because of your great mercy." Today, God is righteous when He extends His mercy to us because His Son Jesus Christ has paid our sin debt [punishment] in full. The Apostle Paul wrote, "He did it to demonstrate his justice at the present time, so as to be just and the one who justifies those who have faith in Jesus" (Romans 3:26).

9:19: This was Daniel's final plea. Daniel was not praying for himself because he had already identified himself with his people when he said, "we have sinned" (verse 15). His plea to God was based upon God's name "sake" and His promises. The prophecy of Jeremiah (from verse 2) was still unfulfilled, as well as the blessings of restoration and re-gathering of his people to the land (Leviticus 26:40 – 45; Deuteronomy 4:29 – 31). Daniel knew all this from his study of the Scriptures, and thus, Daniel understood God's will for His people Israel. For that reason, Daniel appealed to God with the words "do not delay." Daniel's prayer represented his deep concern for God's name sake and for His glory – and even as he prayed, an answer was already on the way.

9:20 – 21: We have already stated that, in his confession to God, Daniel had included himself with his people Israel and their sin. Now we see that Daniel was also, in his words, "confessing my sins." Daniel confessed that he too was a sinner; yet, Daniel was one of those Old Testament patriarchs, like Joseph, in whom we find no sin mentioned in the Scriptures. In fact, recall from chapter 6, that the satraps and administrator tried but could find no corruption or ill conduct in Daniel. The Apostle Paul was correct when he wrote, "For all have sinned and fall short of the glory of God" (Romans 3:23).

Daniel prayed to God for His "holy hill." The holy hill or mountain (KJV) is Jerusalem and the kingdom of God that will be established there (Isaiah 2:1 – 2).

"Gabriel, the man" identifies him with the vision of chapter 8 (verses 15 – 16). Though he was an angel, Gabriel outwardly appeared in human form and here during the "evening sacrifice." The regular daily sacrifices were impossible because of Daniel's exile and the fact that the temple back in Jerusalem laid in ruin. Nevertheless, Daniel continued to observe this ritual by praying during the hour of the evening sacrifice, which would be about 3:00 p.m.

9:22 – 23: Daniel got an immediate answer to his prayer. In fact, Gabriel said that he was sent "as soon as you [Daniel] began to pray." God promises us through the prophet, "Before they call I will answer, while they are speaking I will hear" (Isaiah 65:24). Gabriel also told Daniel that he was "highly esteemed" or, as the KJV states, "greatly beloved" in heaven. How wonderful those words must have sounded to Daniel.

The believer in Jesus Christ is also greatly beloved in heaven. The Apostle Paul, speaking to husbands and wives of their relationship together, likens the husband to Christ and the wife to the church; he writes, "For this reason a man will leave his father and mother and be united to his wife, and the two will become one flesh. This is a profound mystery – but I am talking about Christ and the church" (Ephesians 5:31 – 32). This clearly illustrates that the perfect picture of the relationship between our Lord Jesus Christ and the believer, His church is that of a beloved bride and bridegroom.

The Seventy "Seven" (Weeks)

The prophecy of the seventy "sevens," delivered by Gabriel in these remaining verses is what makes this chapter of such paramount importance in the study of future events related to the nation of Israel.

9:24: Gabriel declared that "Seventy Sevens" or "Seventy Weeks" (KJV) have been decreed.

God's purpose in sending Gabriel was to show Daniel that though his people would be allowed to return to their land at the end of seventy years, it did not mean the restoration of their national dispersion, but only the beginning of a longer period that Gabriel termed "Seventy Sevens." Only at the conclusion of that period would the nation of Israel again be at peace and in control of all the Promised Land. In our context, Daniel had been reading Jeremiah about years – seventy years. Gabriel was sent to explain to Daniel the time necessary to compensate for Israel's violation of seventy sabbatical years; that is, how the nation of Israel neglected to observe the required Sabbath year and allowing their fields and vineyards to lie fallow (Leviticus 25:1 – 7). Consequently, their captivity would likewise be seventy years times seven for a total of 490 years; thus each "seven" of Gabriel's "Seventy Sevens" would represent a period of seven years (just as a decade is a period of 10 years).

1 seven = 7 years

70 sevens = 490 years

This would finally fulfill the words of the prophet: "The land enjoyed its Sabbath rests; all the time of its desolation it rested, until the seventy years were completed in fulfillment of the words of the Lord spoken by Jeremiah" (2 Chronicles 36:21).

Daniel was still troubled as to how the end of the seventy years of captivity fit into God's long range plan including the Gentile world kingdoms which were so blatant in his earlier visions (those of chapters 7 and 8). Daniel must have thought that at the end of the seventy years of exile his people would return to the land, the promised Messiah would appear, and the kingdom of God on earth would be established. Daniel could not reconcile the seemingly conflicting prophecies.

The "Seventy Sevens" gives us the explanation. The seventy sevens for the nation of Israel fit into the "times of the Gentiles" and run parallel with them. The word "decreed," or as the KJV reads, "determined" here means "cutting off." The seventy sevens are broken up in order to fit into gentile times. The "Seventy Sevens" for the nation of Israel and the "times of the Gentiles" both find their conclusion at the second coming of Christ. I cannot stress enough the importance of this fact in correctly understanding this prophecy. The Lord Jesus Christ returns to earth at the end of the last "seven" (the Tribulation Period) to put down all unrighteousness (the Gentile kingdoms) and establish His eternal kingdom on Mount Zion – Jerusalem (for Israel).

"Your people" refers to Daniel's people – the nation of Israel. "Your holy city" refers to Jerusalem. Now according to Gabriel, six purposes are to be accomplished during those seventy sevens, or 490 years:

1) "To finish transgressions." This refers to Israel's transgressions. Christ's death on Calvary's cross provided the redemption for sin, even for the sins of a nation. The word has gone out into the world, but sadly, not all have accepted it. Concerning the last "seven," the prophet

wrote: "And I [God] will pour out on the house of David and the inhabitants of Jerusalem a spirit of grace and supplication …" (Zechariah 12:10).

2) "To put an end to sin." The sins of the nation of Israel will come to an end at the return of Christ. We are all sinners – individually and as a nation, and God will put an end to all sin.

3) "To atone for wickedness." During the seventy sevens, God has provided atonement for both the Jew and Gentile through the sacrificial death and resurrection of His Son Jesus Christ.

4) "To bring in everlasting righteousness" is a clear reference to the return of Christ at the end of the 490 years to establish His eternal kingdom of righteousness.

5) "To seal up vision and prophecy." This refers to the complete fulfillment of all vision and prophecy in Scripture, including the seventy sevens.

6) "To anoint the most holy" refers to the anointment of the Holy of Holies in the Millennial Temple about which the prophet wrote in Ezekiel, chapters 41 – 46.

9:25: The starting point for the Seventy Sevens, this period of 490 years, is crucial in our overall understanding of this prophecy. As I stated earlier, this time period runs parallel with the "times of the Gentiles"; therefore, it must fit into secular history and begin with some date associated with the "times of the Gentiles." As often times is the case with prophecy, there are a number of suggestions as to which Scripture best meets the requirement here which include: the decree of Cyrus (Ezra 1:1 – 4); the decree of Artaxerxes during the seventh year of his reign (Ezra 7:11 – 26); and the decree of Artaxerxes during the twentieth year of his reign (Nehemiah 2:1 – 8). My analysis leans toward the latter decree from Nehemiah. The "decree" or "commandment" (KJV) to restore and rebuild Jerusalem was issued in the month of Nisan, which was the 14th day of March, 445 B.C. – that becomes our starting point.

70 sevens = 490 years

70 sevens divided into 3 periods:

7 sevens + 62 sevens + 1 seven = 70 sevens, or

49 years + 434 years + 7 years = 490 years

The first seven "sevens," or forty-nine years bring us to the end of the Old Testament, 396 B.C. and into the Intertestament Period. These were indeed "times of trouble" as we have already discussed, but the distress was also attested to by both Nehemiah and Malachi.

The next sixty-two "sevens," or 434 years bring us to "Messiah the Prince" (KJV), the "Anointed One," and the day Jesus Christ rode in triumphal entry into Jerusalem, offering Himself for the first time, publicly and officially, as Israel's awaited Messiah – the date was the 2nd day of April (Palm Sunday), A.D. 30.

The simple math tells us that from 445 B.C. to A.D 30 equals 475 years – eight years short of our 483 total years for the combined two periods. How do we reconcile the difference?

First we need to understand that there are years of different lengths: the Lunar year – 354 days; the Calendar year – 360 days; the Solar year – 365 days; and the Julian, or Astronomical year – 365 ¼ days. It is also necessary to add one day every four years to adjust for leap year.

In the account of the flood (Genesis 7:11 and 8:3 – 4), we find that five months were calculated as 150 days, or thirty days to a month, or 360 days to a year. During the end-time seven-year Tribulation

Period (Daniel 9:27), God's two witnesses will prophesy for the first 1,260 days (Revelation 11:3), and then the beast [Antichrist] will kill them and exercise his authority for the final forty-two months (Revelation 13:5 and Daniel 7:25). Each account represents a time period based on a thirty-day month or 360-day year. Clearly, our prophetical chronology should also use a Calendar year of 360 days – for God has been consistent throughout His Word.

To covert from Solar, the commonly used chronology, we start by inclusively counting the years from 445 B.C. to A.D. 30 to arrive at 476 solar years. Next, multiply 476 years by 365 (the number of days in a Solar year) to equal 173,740 days. Now we need to add 119 days to adjust for leap year and twenty days inclusive to adjust from March 14 to April 2, bringing our total to 173,879 days. Lastly, we take our 173,879 days and divide by 360 (the number of days in our prophetical Calendar year) to equal 483 Calendar years. Could there be anything more convincing to prove that Daniel's sixty-nine "sevens" ran out on April 2, A.D. 30, the day our Lord Jesus Christ rode triumphantly into Jerusalem?

Other scholars of biblical prophecy have cited one or the other decrees mentioned above, calculated using either Solar or Lunar calendars, and arrived remarkably close to the date of the beginning of Jesus' public ministry. My major conflict with these explanations is, though John the Baptist testified that Jesus was the "Son of God" (John 1:34) at the beginning of His public ministry, Jesus Himself chose to keep His identity a secret and "strictly warned" his disciples not to tell anyone (Luke 9:21). It was not until the Sunday before His crucifixion, when Jesus rode a donkey into Jerusalem that He offered Himself up publicly as Israel's Messiah (Luke 19:35 – 40). However, if your analysis and conviction lead you to one of these other conclusions, then know that you are in exceedingly good company.

9:26 – 27: There is no time break between the seven sevens and the sixty-two sevens; however, there is a gap – an undetermined time interval between the combined sixty-nine sevens and the final one seven. During this time gap, two very important events are to take place:

1) The "Anointed One," "Messiah" (KJV) will be "cut off and will have nothing," or as the KJV reads, "cut off, but not for himself." This is a clear reference to the rejection and crucifixion of Jesus Christ and the fact that He died "not for himself," but for the sins of the world, all mankind – Jew and Gentile. This is the truth of the gospel and great mystery that the Apostle Paul so often wrote about (Romans 16:25 – 26; Ephesians 3:6). Even after Peter's bold confession that Jesus was "the Christ of God," Jesus tried to explain to him and the other disciples that, "The Son of Man must suffer many things and be rejected by the elders, chief priests and teachers of the law, and he must be killed and on the third day be raised to life" (Luke 9:22). The words of our Lord promise us: "That everyone who believes in him may have eternal life" (John 3:15).

2) The destruction of the "city" – Jerusalem and the "sanctuary" – the temple. In 69 A.D., Titus assumed command of the Roman armies, and one year later, put an end to a four-year Jewish revolt by destroying Jerusalem and the temple in 70 A.D.

Because of Israel's rejection of Jesus as the Messiah, the final "seven," a period of seven years, has been postponed to a future [end] time and thus, remains unfulfilled. This prophetic time gap between the sixty-nine sevens and final seventieth seven is the age of grace – the church age. This time period was kept hidden from the Old Testament prophets (Ephesians 3:1 – 12; 1 Peter 1:10 – 12). Additionally, we are told that during this time interval, the "desolation" of the land of Palestine will continue along with "war" until the "end" comes. The land and those occupying it, will never be at peace until the true Messiah, that is the Lord Jesus Christ, the Prince of Peace returns to establish an everlasting peace.

The "ruler who will come" is a Roman. He will arise out of the revised Roman Empire of the "latter days" (Daniel 2:28 KJV). He is the "little horn" of Daniel 7, the "stern-faced king" of Daniel 8, and the "beast" of Revelation 13 – he is the end-time Antichrist. After the church is removed from the earth at the rapture, he will come onto the scene as a great diplomat and problem solver and "confirm a covenant" (peace treaty) with Israel for "one seven." The signing of this treaty with the nation of Israel starts the prophetic countdown of the final seven years which we refer to as the Tribulation Period. This covenant of peace with Israel is likely the instrument used to allow the rebuilding of the temple and reinstatement of Old Testament worship by the Jewish people. However, in the "middle of the seven," the mid-point of the Tribulation Period, Antichrist breaks his covenant with Israel by putting an "end to sacrifice and offering." He does this by setting up "an abomination that causes desolation," which is a statue of his own image in "the temple" and then demands universal worship by forcing everyone to take his mark – 666 (Revelation 13). The final three and a half years of the seven-year Tribulation Period become the most fearful time of persecution for the Jewish people the world has ever known, and is referred to by our Lord as the "Great Tribulation" (Matthew 24:15 – 26 KJV). As they flee assault from Antichrist, the nation of Israel now realize they missed the first coming of their true Messiah, Jesus Christ and finally turn to Him for salvation. The return of Christ (as Warrior and Judge) to earth at the end of the seven years is the only thing that can put an "end" to the reign of Antichrist and this dreadful period (Matthew 24:27 – 31). The desolation for the nation of Israel and the "times of the Gentiles," both find their conclusion here at the return of Christ, the Rock that will crush all kingdoms and establish a kingdom which will endure forever; as the God of heaven ordained (Daniel 2:44 – 45).

> We are living in the age of grace; and the seventieth seven of Daniel,
> the seven-year Tribulation Period is looming.

Review Questions

1) How did Daniel know that Israel's captivity would last seventy years? _____

   _____.

2) What did we say was the most comprehensive way of determining the will of God? _____

   _____.

3) Name the four basic elements of prayer that Daniel's prayer illustrated: _____

   _____

   _____.

4) Daniel's prayer for the deliverance of his people from their captivity was not based on his or his people's righteousness, but was based on what? _____

   _____.

5) Gabriel's explanation to Daniel of the "Seventy Sevens" was the time necessary to compensate for what? _____.

6) Why is the last "seven" postponed to a future time and what fills the gap in time? _____

   _____.

7) What event starts the prophetic countdown of the final seven-year period and what is this period referred to as? _____

   _____.

Up For Discussion

"I Daniel understood by books [Scriptures] the number of years,
whereof the word of the Lord came to Jeremiah the prophet."
(Daniel 9:2 KJV)

Following this chapter is a one-year Bible Reading Calendar. Are you currently engaged in a tradition of daily Scripture reading? If so, how has it impacted your life and your daily Christian walk? Why is it important for believers to read and study God's Word daily?

Do more: Copy and share the Bible Reading Calendar with others. Make it your ministry!

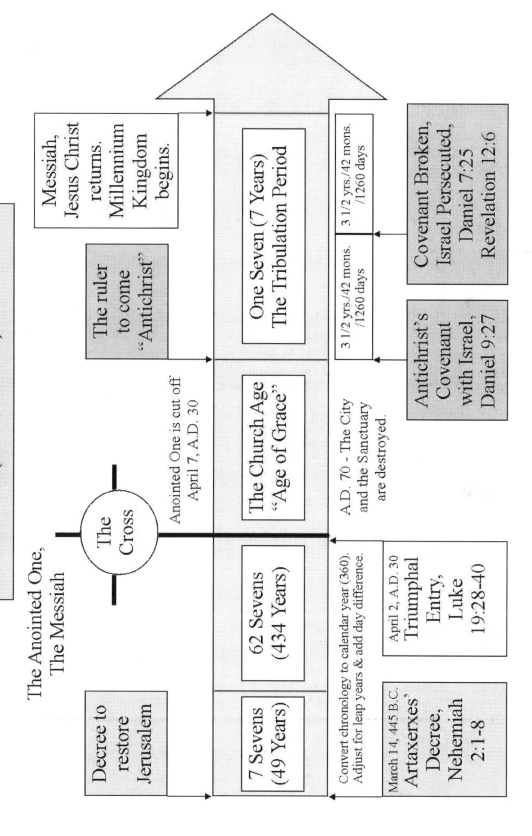

Daniel's "Seventy Sevens"
(Daniel 9:24-27)

The Anointed One, The Messiah

Decree to restore Jerusalem

Messiah, Jesus Christ returns. Millennium Kingdom begins.

The ruler to come "Antichrist"

Anointed One is cut off April 7, A.D. 30

The Cross

The Church Age "Age of Grace"

One Seven (7 Years) The Tribulation Period

3 1/2 yrs./42 mons. /1260 days

3 1/2 yrs./42 mons. /1260 days

Covenant Broken, Israel Persecuted, Daniel 7:25 Revelation 12:6

Antichrist's Covenant with Israel, Daniel 9:27

A.D. 70 - The City and the Sanctuary are destroyed.

62 Sevens (434 Years)

7 Sevens (49 Years)

Convert chronology to calendar year (360). Adjust for leap years & add day difference.

April 2, A.D. 30 Triumphal Entry, Luke 19:28-40

March 14, 445 B.C. Artaxerxes' Decree, Nehemiah 2:1-8

The Abomination That Causes Desolation

Matthew 24:15: "So when you see standing in the Holy Place the abomination that causes desolation, spoken of through the prophet Daniel – let the reader understand."

Mark 13:14: "When you see the abomination that causes desolation standing where it does not belong – let the reader understand – then let those who are in Judea flee to the mountains."

Luke 21:20: "When you see Jerusalem being surrounded by armies, you will know that its desolation is near."

An abomination is defined in our Bible dictionary as anything that offends the spiritual, religious, or moral sense of a person and causes extreme disgust.

The "abomination that causes desolation" is a despicable misuse of the Jewish Temple during a time of great distress.

This phrase is found in both the gospels of Matthew and Mark and again alluded to in Luke, as cited above. These are the words of our Lord Jesus Christ as He quoted from Daniel in His discourse to the disciples concerning the end of the age. In Daniel, the words literally mean "the abomination that makes desolate." In other words, Daniel prophesied that the Temple would be used for an "abominable" purpose at some time in the future. As a result, God's faithful people (Daniel's people) would no longer worship there – so great would be their moral revulsion at the sacrilege, that the Temple would become "desolate."

The Book of Daniel introduces us to the doctrine of dual reference – a prophecy that has its fulfillment in the immediate future and a second like-manner fulfillment in the distant future. In his visions, Daniel saw two kings, both he referred to as a "little horn" who grew in power to persecute his people – Israel. The little horn of Daniel's vision in chapter 8 grew out of the fragmented empire of Greece after the death of Alexander the Great (Daniel's immediate future), whereby the little horn of Daniel's vision in chapter 7 grew out of the revised Roman Empire of the latter days (the distant future).

Daniel used the phrase "the abomination that causes desolation" three times in connection with these kings:

"His armed forces will rise up to desecrate the temple fortress and will abolish the daily sacrifice. Then they will set up the abomination that causes desolation" (Daniel 11:31).

This prophecy was fulfilled by Antiochus IV Epiphanes, who was, without a doubt, the cruelest ruler of Syria and Palestine under the Seleucid Empire of Greece. Upon returning from war with Egypt and a humiliating withdrawal imposed by the Romans in 168 B.C., Antiochus directly proceeded to unleash his rage against Israel. He broke his truce with the Jews by siding with the Hellenized faction and attacked Jerusalem with intense fury. He "abolished the daily sacrifice" by outlawing all Jewish religious rites and traditions. He then desecrated the temple by setting up the "abomination that causes desolation," which was an image of the Greek god Zeus erected in the Holy Place and commanded everyone to worship the Olympian god. If that wasn't enough, he then sacrificed swine (pigs – an unclean animal to the Jews) on the Altar of Burned Offerings. The Jewish resistance was met by the slaughter of countless thousands and the destruction of their city, Jerusalem.

However, Antiochus Epiphanes was merely a foreshadowing of the king who is coming at the time of the end – the distant future. He is Antichrist. The end-time Antichrist will do on a much greater scale what Antiochus, by contrast, did in miniature.

"He will confirm a covenant with many for one 'seven.' In the middle of the 'seven' he will put an end to sacrifice and offering. On a wing of the temple he will set up an abomination that causes desolation, until the end that is decreed is poured out on him" (Daniel 9:27).

"From the time that the daily sacrifice is abolished and the abomination that causes desolation is set up, there will be 1,290 days" (Daniel 12:11).

These two prophecies refer to the end-time Antichrist and are yet unfulfilled. After all Christians are removed from the earth (called home to be with Christ in heaven) at the rapture, the world and those left behind will be in a state of chaos. Antichrist will emerge onto the world stage and conquer the troubled hearts of the people by diplomacy, promising peace and prosperity. He will sign a seven-year treaty of peace with "many," including the nation of Israel, thus triggering the seven-year Tribulation Period described in the Book of Revelation. This covenant will likely include terms that allow the temple in Jerusalem to be rebuilt and the re-instatement of traditional Jewish ritual and worship. He will be the one who then puts the Roman Empire back together as he rises to power and ultimately becomes ruler of the united world during the first three and a half years. However, in the "middle" of the seven years, Antichrist will break his covenant with Israel by putting an "end to sacrifice and offering." He does this by setting up "an abomination that causes desolation," which is a statue of his own image in "the temple" and then demands universal worship by forcing everyone to take his mark – 666 (Revelation 13). The final three and a half years of the seven-year Tribulation Period become the most fearful time of persecution for the Jewish people the world has ever known, and is referred to by our Lord Jesus Christ as the "Great Tribulation" (Matthew 24:15 – 26 KJV).

Antichrist's rule will come to an abrupt end at the conclusion of the Tribulation Period when Christ returns to earth to conquer and abolish all wickedness and establishes His everlasting kingdom of righteousness.

Daniel said that both rulers would be "destroyed, but not by human power" (Daniel 8:25). Antiochus Epiphanes died of a painful disease while in Persia in 164 B.C. Antichrist will be defeated and destroyed by the spoken Word of God when Christ returns to earth as Warrior and Judge at the end of the age.

Bible Reading Calendar

JANUARY

Date	Morning	Evening	Date	Morning	Evening
1	Gen. 1, 2	Matt. 1	17	Gen. 41	Matt. 13:1-32
2	Gen. 3, 4, 5	Matt. 2	18	Gen. 42, 43	Matt. 13:33-58
3	Gen. 6, 7, 8	Matt. 3	19	Gen. 44, 45	Matt. 14:1-21
4	Gen. 9, 10, 11	Matt. 4	20	Gen. 46, 47, 48	Matt. 14:22-36
5	Gen. 12, 13, 14	Matt. 5:1-26	21	Gen. 49, 50	Matt. 15:1-20
6	Gen. 15, 16, 17	Matt. 5:27-48	22	Exod. 1, 2, 3	Matt. 15:21-39
7	Gen. 18, 19	Matt. 6	23	Exod. 4, 5, 6	Matt. 16
8	Gen. 20, 21, 22	Matt. 7	24	Exod. 7, 8	Matt. 17
9	Gen. 23, 24	Matt. 8	25	Exod. 9, 10	Matt. 18:1-20
10	Gen. 25, 26	Matt. 9:1-17	26	Exod. 11, 12	Matt. 18:21-35
11	Gen. 27, 28	Matt. 9:18-38	27	Exod. 13, 14, 15	Matt. 19:1-15
12	Gen. 29, 30	Matt. 10:1-23	28	Exod. 16, 17, 18	Matt. 19:16-30
13	Gen. 31, 32	Matt. 10:24-42	29	Exod. 19, 20, 21	Matt. 20:1-16
14	Gen. 33, 34, 35	Matt. 11	30	Exod. 22, 23, 24	Matt. 20:17-34
15	Gen. 36, 37	Matt. 12:1-21	31	Exod. 25, 26	Matt. 21:1-22
16	Gen. 38, 39, 40	Matt. 12:22-50			

FEBRUARY

Date	Morning	Evening	Date	Morning	Evening
1	Exod. 27, 28	Matt. 21:23-46	17	Lev. 24, 25	Mark 1:23-45
2	Exod. 29, 30	Matt. 22:1-22	18	Lev. 26, 27	Mark 2
3	Exod. 31, 32, 33	Matt. 22:23-46	19	Num. 1, 2	Mark 3:1-21
4	Exod. 34, 35, 36	Matt. 23:1-22	20	Num. 3, 4	Mark 3:22-35
5	Exod. 37, 38	Matt. 23:23-39	21	Num. 5, 6	Mark 4:1-20
6	Exod. 39, 40	Matt. 24:1-22	22	Num. 7	Mark 4:21-41
7	Lev. 1, 2, 3	Matt. 24:23-51	23	Num. 8, 9, 10	Mark 5:1-20
8	Lev. 4, 5, 6	Matt. 25:1-30	24	Num. 11, 12, 13	Mark 5:21-43
9	Lev. 7, 8, 9	Matt. 25:31-46	25	Num. 14, 15	Mark 6:1-32
10	Lev. 10, 11, 12	Matt. 26:1-19	26	Num. 16, 17	Mark 6:33-56
11	Lev. 13	Matt. 26:20-54	27	Num. 18, 19, 20	Mark 7:1-13
12	Lev. 14, 15	Matt. 26:55-75	28	Num. 21, 22	Mark 7:14-37
13	Lev. 16, 17	Matt. 27:1-31	29	Num. 23, 24, 25	Mark 8:1-21
14	Lev. 18, 19	Matt. 27:32-66	Divide chapters for February 29 and read them		
15	Lev. 20, 21	Matt. 28	February 28 and March 1		
16	Lev. 22, 23	Mark 1:1-22	when February has only 28 days.		

MARCH

Date	Morning	Evening	Date	Morning	Evening
1	Num. 26, 27	Mark 8:22-38	17	Deut. 29, 30	Mark 16
2	Num. 28, 29	Mark 9:1-29	18	Deut. 31, 32	Luke 1:1-23
3	Num. 30, 31	Mark 9:30-50	19	Deut. 33, 34	Luke 1:24-56
4	Num. 32, 33	Mark 10:1-31	20	Joshua 1, 2, 3	Luke 1:57-80
5	Num. 34, 35, 36	Mark 10:32-52	21	Joshua 4, 5, 6	Luke 2:1-24
6	Deut. 1, 2	Mark 11:1-19	22	Joshua 7, 8	Luke 2:25-52
7	Deut. 3, 4	Mark 11:20-33	23	Joshua 9, 10	Luke 3
8	Deut. 5, 6, 7	Mark 12:1-27	24	Joshua 11, 12, 13	Luke 4:1-32
9	Deut. 8, 9, 10	Mark 12:28-44	25	Joshua 14, 15	Luke 4:33-44
10	Deut. 11, 12, 13	Mark 13:1-13	26	Joshua 16, 17, 18	Luke 5:1-16
11	Deut. 14, 15, 16	Mark 13:14-37	27	Joshua 19, 20	Luke 5:17-39
12	Deut. 17, 18, 19	Mark 14:1-25	28	Joshua 21, 22	Luke 6:1-26
13	Deut. 20, 21, 22	Mark 14:26-50	29	Joshua 23, 24	Luke 6:27-49
14	Deut. 23, 24, 25	Mark 14:51-72	30	Judges 1, 2	Luke 7:1-30
15	Deut. 26, 27	Mark 15:1-26	31	Judges 3, 4, 5	Luke 7:31-50
16	Deut. 28	Mark 15:27-47			

"Till I come, give attendance to reading, to exhortation, to doctrine."
1 Timothy 4:13

APRIL

Date	Morning	Evening	Date	Morning	Evening
1	Judges 6, 7	Luke 8:1-21	17	I Sam. 22, 23, 24	Luke 16:1-18
2	Judges 8, 9	Luke 8:22-56	18	I Sam. 25, 26	Luke 16:19-31
3	Judges 10, 11	Luke 9:1-36	19	I Sam. 27, 28, 29	Luke 17:1-19
4	Judges 12, 13, 14	Luke 9:37-62	20	I Sam. 30, 31	Luke 17:20-37
5	Judges 15, 16, 17	Luke 10:1-24	21	II Sam. 1, 2, 3	Luke 18:1-17
6	Judges 18, 19	Luke 10:25-42	22	II Sam. 4, 5, 6	Luke 18:18-43
7	Judges 20, 21	Luke 11:1-28	23	II Sam. 7, 8, 9	Luke 19:1-28
8	Ruth 1, 2, 3, 4	Luke 11:29-54	24	II Sam. 10, 11, 12	Luke 19:29-48
9	I Sam. 1, 2, 3	Luke 12:1-34	25	II Sam. 13, 14	Luke 20:1-26
10	I Sam. 4, 5, 6	Luke 12:35-59	26	II Sam. 15, 16	Luke 20:27-47
11	I Sam. 7, 8, 9	Luke 13:1-21	27	II Sam. 17, 18	Luke 21:1-19
12	I Sam. 10, 11, 12	Luke 13:22-35	28	II Sam. 19, 20	Luke 21:20-38
13	I Sam. 13, 14	Luke 14:1-24	29	II Sam. 21, 22	Luke 22:1-30
14	I Sam. 15, 16	Luke 14:25-35	30	II Sam. 23, 24	Luke 22:31-53
15	I Sam. 17, 18	Luke 15:1-10			
16	I Sam. 19, 20, 21	Luke 15:11-32			

MAY

Date	Morning	Evening	Date	Morning	Evening
1	I Kings 1, 2	Luke 22:54-71	17	II Kings 18, 19	John 6:22-44
2	I Kings 3, 4, 5	Luke 23:1-26	18	II Kings 20, 21, 22	John 6:45-71
3	I Kings 6, 7	Luke 23:27-38	19	II Kings 23, 24, 25	John 7:1-31
4	I Kings 8, 9	Luke 23:39-56	20	I Chron. 1, 2	John 7:32-53
5	I Kings 10, 11	Luke 24:1-35	21	I Chron. 3, 4, 5	John 8:1-20
6	I Kings 12, 13	Luke 24:36-53	22	I Chron. 6, 7	John 8:21-36
7	I Kings 14, 15	John 1:1-28	23	I Chron. 8, 9, 10	John 8:37-59
8	I Kings 16, 17, 18	John 1:29-51	24	I Chron. 11, 12, 13	John 9:1-23
9	I Kings 19, 20	John 2	25	I Chron. 14, 15, 16	John 9:24-41
10	I Kings 21, 22	John 3:1-21	26	I Chron. 17, 18, 19	John 10:1-21
11	II Kings 1, 2, 3	John 3:22-36	27	I Chron. 20, 21, 22	John 10:22-42
12	II Kings 4, 5	John 4:1-30	28	I Chron. 23, 24, 25	John 11:1-17
13	II Kings 6, 7, 8	John 4:31-54	29	I Chron. 26, 27	John 11:18-46
14	II Kings 9, 10, 11	John 5:1-24	30	I Chron. 28, 29	John 11:47-57
15	II Kings 12, 13, 14	John 5:25-47	31	II Chr. 1, 2, 3	John 12:1-19
16	II Kings 15, 16, 17	John 6:1-21			

JUNE

Date	Morning	Evening	Date	Morning	Evening
1	II Chr. 4, 5, 6	John 12:20-50	17	Neh. 4, 5, 6	Acts 2:14-47
2	II Chr. 7, 8, 9	John 13:1-17	18	Neh. 7, 8	Acts 3
3	II Chr. 10, 11, 12	John 13:18-38	19	Neh. 9, 10, 11	Acts 4:1-22
4	II Chr. 13-16	John 14	20	Neh. 12, 13	Acts 4:23-37
5	II Chr. 17, 18, 19	John 15	21	Esther 1, 2, 3	Acts 5:1-16
6	II Chr. 20, 21, 22	John 16:1-15	22	Esther 4, 5, 6	Acts 5:17-42
7	II Chr. 23, 24, 25	John 16:16-33	23	Esther 7-10	Acts 6
8	II Chr. 26, 27, 28	John 17	24	Job 1, 2, 3	Acts 7:1-19
9	II Chr. 29, 30, 31	John 18:1-23	25	Job 4, 5, 6	Acts 7:20-43
10	II Chr. 32, 33, 34	John 18:24-40	26	Job 7, 8, 9	Acts 7:44-60
11	II Chr. 35, 36	John 19:1-22	27	Job 10, 11, 12	Acts 8:1-25
12	Ezra 1, 2	John 19:23-42	28	Job 13, 14, 15	Acts 8:26-40
13	Ezra 3, 4, 5	John 20	29	Job 16, 17, 18	Acts 9:1-22
14	Ezra 6, 7, 8	John 21	30	Job 19, 20	Acts 9:23-43
15	Ezra 9, 10	Acts 1			
16	Neh. 1, 2, 3	Acts 2:1-13			

JULY

Date	Morning	Evening	Date	Morning	Evening
1	Job 21, 22	Acts 10:1-23	17	Psalm 22, 23, 24	Acts 20:1-16
2	Job 23, 24, 25	Acts 10:24-48	18	Psalm 25, 26, 27	Acts 20:17-38
3	Job 26, 27, 28	Acts 11	19	Psalm 28, 29, 30	Acts 21:1-14
4	Job 29, 30	Acts 12	20	Psalm 31, 32, 33	Acts 21:15-40
5	Job 31, 32	Acts 13:1-23	21	Psalm 34, 35	Acts 22
6	Job 33, 34	Acts 13:24-52	22	Psalm 36, 37	Acts 23:1-11
7	Job 35, 36, 37	Acts 14	23	Psalm 38, 39, 40	Acts 23:12-35
8	Job 38, 39	Acts 15:1-21	24	Psalm 41, 42, 43	Acts 24
9	Job 40, 41, 42	Acts 15:22-41	25	Psalm 44, 45, 46	Acts 25
10	Psalm 1, 2, 3	Acts 16:1-15	26	Psalm 47, 48, 49	Acts 26
11	Psalm 4, 5, 6	Acts 16:16-40	27	Psalm 50, 51, 52	Acts 27:1-25
12	Psalm 7, 8, 9	Acts 17:1-15	28	Psalm 53, 54, 55	Acts 27:26-44
13	Psalm 10, 11, 12	Acts 17:16-34	29	Psalm 56, 57, 58	Acts 28:1-15
14	Psalm 13, 14, 15, 16	Acts 18	30	Psalm 59, 60, 61	Acts 28:16-31
15	Psalm 17, 18	Acts 19:1-20	31	Psalm 62, 63, 64	Rom. 1
16	Psalm 19, 20, 21	Acts 19:21-41			

AUGUST

Date	Morning	Evening	Date	Morning	Evening
1	Psalm 65, 66, 67	Rom. 2	17	Psalm 107, 108	Rom. 15:21-33
2	Psalm 68, 69	Rom. 3	18	Psalm 109, 110, 111	Rom. 16
3	Psalm 70, 71, 72	Rom. 4	19	Psalm 112-115	I Cor. 1
4	Psalm 73, 74	Rom. 5	20	Psalm 116-118	I Cor. 2
5	Psalm 75, 76, 77	Rom. 6	21	Psalm 119:1-48	I Cor. 3
6	Psalm 78	Rom. 7	22	Psalm 119:49-104	I Cor. 4
7	Psalm 79, 80, 81	Rom. 8:1-18	23	Psalm 119:105-176	I Cor. 5
8	Psalm 82, 83, 84	Rom. 8:19-39	24	Psalm 120-123	I Cor. 6
9	Psalm 85, 86, 87	Rom. 9	25	Psalm 124-127	I Cor. 7:1-24
10	Psalm 88, 89	Rom. 10	26	Psalm 128-131	I Cor. 7:25-40
11	Psalm 90, 91, 92	Rom. 11:1-21	27	Psalm 132-135	I Cor. 8
12	Psalm 93, 94, 95	Rom. 11:22-36	28	Psalm 136-138	I Cor. 9
13	Psalm 96, 97, 98	Rom. 12	29	Psalm 139-141	I Cor. 10:1-13
14	Psalm 99-102	Rom. 13	30	Psalm 142-144	I Cor. 10:14-33
15	Psalm 103, 104	Rom. 14	31	Psalm 145-147	I Cor. 11:1-15
16	Psalm 105, 106	Rom. 15:1-20			

SEPTEMBER

Date	Morning	Evening	Date	Morning	Evening
1	Psalm 148-150	I Cor. 11:16-34	17	Eccles. 1, 2, 3	II Cor. 9
2	Proverbs 1, 2	I Cor. 12	18	Eccles. 4, 5, 6	II Cor. 10
3	Proverbs 3, 4	I Cor. 13	19	Eccles. 7, 8, 9	II Cor. 11:1-15
4	Proverbs 5, 6	I Cor. 14:1-20	20	Eccles. 10, 11, 12	II Cor. 11:16-33
5	Proverbs 7, 8	I Cor. 14:21-40	21	Songs 1, 2, 3	II Cor. 12
6	Proverbs 9, 10	I Cor. 15:1-32	22	Songs 4, 5	II Cor. 13
7	Proverbs 11, 12	I Cor. 15:33-58	23	Songs 6, 7, 8	Gal. 1
8	Proverbs 13, 14	I Cor. 16	24	Isaiah 1, 2, 3	Gal. 2
9	Proverbs 15, 16	II Cor. 1	25	Isaiah 4, 5, 6	Gal. 3
10	Proverbs 17, 18	II Cor. 2	26	Isaiah 7, 8, 9	Gal. 4
11	Proverbs 19, 20	II Cor. 3	27	Isaiah 10, 11, 12	Gal. 5
12	Proverbs 21, 22	II Cor. 4	28	Isaiah 13, 14, 15	Gal. 6
13	Proverbs 23, 24	II Cor. 5	29	Isaiah 16, 17, 18	Eph. 1
14	Proverbs 25, 26, 27	II Cor. 6	30	Isaiah 19, 20, 21	Eph. 2
15	Proverbs 28, 29	II Cor. 7			
16	Proverbs 30, 31	II Cor. 8			

"Meditate upon these things, give thyself wholly to them…"						
1 Timothy 4:15						

OCTOBER

Date	Morning		Evening		Date	Morning		Evening	
1	Isaiah	22, 23	Eph.	3	17	Isaiah	62, 63, 64	I Thess.	5
2	Isaiah	24, 25, 26	Eph.	4	18	Isaiah	65, 66	II Thess.	1
3	Isaiah	27, 28	Eph.	5	19	Jer.	1, 2	II Thess.	2
4	Isaiah	29, 30	Eph.	6	20	Jer.	3, 4	II Thess.	3
5	Isaiah	31, 32, 33	Phil.	1	21	Jer.	5, 6	I Tim.	1
6	Isaiah	34, 35, 36	Phil.	2	22	Jer.	7, 8	I Tim.	2
7	Isaiah	37, 38	Phil.	3	23	Jer.	9, 10	I Tim.	3
8	Isaiah	39, 40	Phil.	4	24	Jer.	11, 12, 13	I Tim.	4
9	Isaiah	41, 42	Col.	1	25	Jer.	14, 15, 16	I Tim.	5
10	Isaiah	43, 44	Col.	2	26	Jer.	17, 18, 19	I Tim.	6
11	Isaiah	45, 46, 47	Col.	3	27	Jer.	20, 21, 22	II Tim.	1
12	Isaiah	48, 49	Col.	4	28	Jer.	23, 24	II Tim.	2
13	Isaiah	50, 51, 52	I Thess.	1	29	Jer.	25, 26	II Tim.	3
14	Isaiah	53, 54, 55	I Thess.	2	30	Jer.	27, 28	II Tim.	4
15	Isaiah	56, 57, 58	I Thess.	3	31	Jer.	29, 30	Titus	1
16	Isaiah	59, 60, 61	I Thess.	4					

NOVEMBER

Date	Morning		Evening		Date	Morning		Evening	
1	Jer.	31, 32	Titus	2	17	Ezek.	16	Hebrews	12
2	Jer.	33, 34, 35	Titus	3	18	Ezek.	17, 18, 19	Hebrews	13
3	Jer.	36, 37	Philemon		19	Ezek.	20, 21	James	1
4	Jer.	38, 39	Hebrews	1	20	Ezek.	22, 23	James	2
5	Jer.	40, 41, 42	Hebrews	2	21	Ezek.	24, 25, 26	James	3
6	Jer.	43, 44, 45	Hebrews	3	22	Ezek.	27, 28	James	4
7	Jer.	46, 47, 48	Hebrews	4	23	Ezek.	29, 30, 31	James	5
8	Jer.	49, 50	Hebrews	5	24	Ezek.	32, 33	I Peter	1
9	Jer.	51, 52	Hebrews	6	25	Ezek.	34, 35	I Peter	2
10	Lam.	1, 2	Hebrews	7	26	Ezek.	36, 37	I Peter	3
11	Lam.	3, 4, 5	Hebrews	8	27	Ezek.	38, 39	I Peter	4
12	Ezek.	1, 2, 3	Hebrews	9	28	Ezek.	40	I Peter	5
13	Ezek	4, 5, 6	Hebrews	10:1-23	29	Ezek.	41, 42	II Peter	1
14	Ezek.	7, 8, 9	Hebrews	10:24-39	30	Ezek.	43, 44	II Peter	2
15	Ezek.	10, 11, 12	Hebrews	11:1-19					
16	Ezek	13, 14, 15	Hebrews	11:20-40					

DECEMBER

Date	Morning		Evening		Date	Morning		Evening	
1	Ezek.	45, 46	II Peter	3	17	Obadiah		Rev.	8
2	Ezek.	47, 48	I John	1	18	Jonah		Rev.	9
3	Dan.	1, 2	I John	2	19	Micah	1, 2, 3	Rev.	10
4	Dan.	3, 4	I John	3	20	Micah	4, 5	Rev.	11
5	Dan.	5, 6	I John	4	21	Micah	6, 7	Rev.	12
6	Dan	7, 8	I John	5	22	Nahum		Rev.	13
7	Dan.	9, 10	II John		23	Habakkuk		Rev.	14
8	Dan.	11, 12	III John		24	Zephaniah		Rev.	15
9	Hosea	1-4	Jude		25	Haggai		Rev.	16
10	Hosea	5-8	Rev.	1	26	Zech.	1, 2, 3	Rev.	17
11	Hosea	9, 10, 11	Rev.	2	27	Zech.	4, 5, 6	Rev.	18
12	Hosea	12, 13, 14	Rev.	3	28	Zech.	7, 8, 9	Rev.	19
13	Joel		Rev.	4	29	Zech.	10, 11, 12	Rev.	20
14	Amos	1, 2, 3	Rev.	5	30	Zech.	13, 14	Rev.	21
15	Amos	4, 5, 6	Rev.	6	31	Malachi		Rev.	22
16	Amos	7, 8, 9	Rev.	7					

Chapter 10

This last vision of Daniel's extends through our final three chapters of the book. The vision tells of events exclusively related to the nation of Israel in Daniel's immediate future as well as the distant future of the "latter days" (2:28). We have already seen the notion of dual reference, a prophecy with its imminent fulfillment that in turn, gives us helpful understanding as a foreshadowing of its second future fulfillment. The two "little horns" we have previously looked at are an example of this; one fulfilled historically in Antiochus IV Epiphanes, thus foreshadowing in type the one still to come in the latter days, Antichrist. This vision also gives us some added details of earlier visions. Though all the visions were prophetic at the time they were given to Daniel, much has already come to pass and recorded in our secular history. There is also much that yet awaits its fulfillment in the future at the time of the end; however, the line that separates fulfilled from unfulfilled is not always clear, as we will see.

We are also moving into a brief section, little known and unnerving to us, where we will get a glimpse into the spiritual world. We are given just enough information on this unseen world of spiritual warfare to produce a sobering effect on us, much the same as it did on Daniel. This will acquaint us somewhat with the order of angels, both good and bad (fallen). Angels, like man, evidently have free will; consequently, we are told that one-third of the angels in heaven chose to follow Satan in rebellion to God (Revelation 12:4).

Before we get started with our chapter commentary, let's take a brief look into what theologians say about angels including some Scriptural references. The Apostle Paul, when explaining the supremacy of Christ, gives us a partial break-down of the hierarchy of the created heavenly host, angels: "For by him were all things created, that are in heaven, and that are in earth, visible and invisible, whether they be thrones, or dominions, or principalities, or powers: all things were created by him, and for him" (Colossians 1:16 KJV). There exists a great invisible realm and heavenly order that, to mankind, is largely speculative:

Seraphim are thought to be the highest order and serve as attendants to the throne of God (Isaiah 6:1 – 3; Revelation 4:6 – 8). Cherubim are the next order and are closely linked with God's glory and knowledge. Cherubim, manlike in their appearance, were stationed on the eastern borders to guard the Garden of Eden (Genesis 3:24), and their image was crafted onto the atonement cover of the Ark of the Covenant (Exodus 25:17 – 20). The prophet described the cherubim in his vision as having four faces (Ezekiel 10:14). Thrones are the third closest to God, and it is suggested that they serve as God's chariot and are described as "wheels … full of eyes" (Ezekiel 1:15 – 18). Dominions are said to regulate the duties of lower angels. The principalities carry out their orders and oversee groups of people. Virtues are said to be responsible for the movement of the heavenly bodies and the forces of nature (Revelation 7:1). The powers would be the warrior angels that fight for humanity against the demonic spirits. The archangels, Michael and Gabriel (and allegedly five others totaling seven) are portrayed as "chief or leading angels." Michael is the chief commander of God's heavenly army (Revelation 12:7), and also the "great prince" who serves as protector of the nation of Israel (Daniel 12:1) and supposedly the church since the time of the apostles. Gabriel is God's special herald, illustrated by his announcements to Daniel concerning the prophecy of the Seventy Sevens (Daniel 9:21 – 27), to Zechariah concerning the birth of John the Baptist (Luke 1:11 – 19), and to the Virgin Mary to proclaim the birth of our Lord and Savior Jesus Christ (Luke 1:26 – 31). The "mighty" angels of Revelation 5:2 and 10:1 may also be archangels. Archangels are considered by some theologians as equal in status to seraphim, or even themselves' seraphim. The lowest and most recognized order is "plain" angel. They are the closest to the material world and mankind. Our guardian angels may fall into either this last category or the above mentioned powers (Matthew 18:10).

One-third of these celestial beings fell away in rebellion to follow Satan and now belong to the order of demons to which frequent mention is made throughout the gospels. Satan has organized his demons into an order of rank as well; and again the Apostle Paul explains: "For we wrestle not against flesh and blood, but against principalities, against powers, against the rulers of the darkness of this world, against spiritual wickedness in high places" (Ephesians 6:12 KJV). We have already mentioned the principalities and powers. In addition, Satan's ranks include the rulers of the "darkness of the world." These would be comparable in Satan's order to archangels in God's heavenly order; one is even mentioned by name – Abaddon (Revelation 9:11). Lastly, there are the rulers of the "spiritual wickedness in high places," referring to those demons in charge of promoting religion – Satan's religion in opposition to Christ. This is a religion of lies and deception and often includes the use of miraculous signs (Revelation 16:13 – 14).

Both groups, angels and demons, exist and operate in the "invisible" realm around us. They are engaged in ceaseless warfare – spiritual warfare to win over the hearts and souls of men.

10:1: The "third year of Cyrus king of Persia" refers to the third year after his conquest of Babylon in 539 B.C., thus making the year 536 B.C. This would be within two or three years after Daniel's vision of the Seventy Sevens. By this time, Daniel was an old man well into his eighties and likely retired from the king's service. He had lived through the entire seventy-year Babylonian/Persian captivity.

A "revelation," or as the KJV simply refers to a "thing," was a new message revealed to Daniel. Daniel said it was "true" and that its "understanding" was made clear to him in this final vision. However, because of a "great war," meaning spiritual war (mentioned above), the time "appointed was long" (KJV) meaning that its fulfillment was in the distant future, not imminent.

10:2 – 3: We were not told why Daniel mourned, but we can make some educated conjecture based on the Scriptures. Yes, Daniel desired to understand the vision and humbled himself (verse 12), but even more I believe Daniel grieved for his people. Three years earlier, in the first year of his reign, Cyrus issued the decree which allowed the Jews to return to their home land under Zerubbabel to rebuild the temple in Jerusalem (Ezra 1:1 – 4). Sadly, less than 43,000 Jews, an insignificant few, made the journey. The vast majority of Jews were content to remain behind in the pagan Persian

Empire as immigrants. This was a source of grief to the aged prophet to see that his people did not want to return to their home land.

"Until the three weeks were over" refers to Daniel's preparation and observance of the Passover and the Feast of Unleavened Bread which occurred during the first month (verse 4) of the year (Leviticus 23:5 – 8).

10:4: Daniel has given us the date that he received his vision and message as "the twenty-fourth day of the first month," which was three days following the Unleavened Bread festival in the month of Nisan, or our April. Daniel has also told us exactly where he was at the time – the banks of the Tigris River, not at his former residence in Babylon. The Tigris River flows east of and roughly parallel to the Euphrates River until the two join in the marshes about 40 miles north of the Persian Gulf. It is also described as one of the four headwaters that flowed from the Garden of Eden (Genesis 2:14). Daniel has given us an exact date in these opening verses. This may be God's way of silencing those who would later challenge His prophet's authorship.

Daniel's Vision of the Glorified Christ

10:5 – 6: Daniel's last vision began like none of his earlier visions. This was a new revelation or method of conveying a message. This vision contained no image or vision of beasts or years of sevens. Daniel's final revelation began with the vision of "a man dressed in linen . . . ." As a student of prophecy and God's Word, there can be no doubt in my mind that what Daniel witnessed was the Person of Christ – the Son of God. We have already seen the pre-incarnate Christ working through Daniel in previous chapters; however, in this vision of Christ, Daniel did not see Him as pre-incarnate, but rather as post-incarnate – as the glorified Christ – Jesus Christ after His ascension into glory. Daniel's vision strikingly parallels the vision given to the Apostle John: "I turned around to see the voice that was speaking to me. And when I turned I saw seven golden lampstands, and among the lampstands was someone 'like a son of man,' dressed in a robe reaching to his feet and with a golden sash around his chest. His head and hair were white like wool, as white as snow, and his eyes were like blazing fire. His feet were like bronze glowing in a furnace, and his voice was like the sound of rushing waters" (Revelation 1:12 – 15).

It is of utmost importance for us to note here that Daniel's final vision (contained in these remaining three chapters) and the Apostle John's vision in the Book of Revelation both begin remarkably in the very same manner – with a vision of the Risen Lord, Jesus Christ. That would suggest to us today that the prophecies contained in both visions represent the most significant prophecies of end-time events to be found in the Word of God. Both visions find their fulfillment with the return of Christ to earth to establish His eternal kingdom; and thus, Christ gives both prophets His personal endorsement.

10:7 – 9: Although there were other men with Daniel, only he saw the vision. The Apostle Paul had a similar experience on the road to Damascus: "The men traveling with Saul stood there speechless; they heard the sound but did not see anyone" (Acts 9:7). Paul, however, fell to the ground and was blinded by the vision of the glorified Christ. The vision of Christ had a transforming effect on Daniel, physically, as well it should. The effect was similar to, but obviously more intense than his first encounter with the angel Gabriel. Daniel became "helpless," his "strength left" him, and his "face turned deathly pale." As a result of John's vision of Christ, the apostle said that he "fell at his feet as though dead" (Revelation 1:17). Humans simply cannot stand in the holy presence of God.

"I was left alone, gazing at this great vision." How awesome and wonderful this must have been. This experience is shared throughout the Scriptures with other godly men, from Abraham to Moses, Elijah, John the Baptist, the Apostle Paul, to the Apostle John imprisoned on the island of Patmos – God was with them all. I get up early every morning to spend some quiet and peaceful time alone with the Lord in prayer and in His Word. I cannot think of a better way to begin each day. It is a special time for me, and it is the time when God speaks most directly to me. How else can we know what God desires for each of us unless we spend time alone with Him each day? It had a tremendous effect on Daniel, and I assure you, it will have a similar effect on you.

Daniel "fell into a deep sleep" means that Daniel abruptly lost consciousness; kind of like being given anesthesia before an operation – one moment you are awake and the next you are deep in sleep. For how long we do not know; however, when he awoke the Lord Jesus had left and an angel had come to minister to him.

The Angelic Messenger

10:10 – 11: As Daniel laid "face to the ground" a "hand touched" him and brought him "trembling" to his "hands and knees." This was the hand of an angel sent by Christ to answer Daniel's prayer request. We are not told the identity of this angel; but because of the significance of the message, many believe the angel was likely Gabriel, since he had been sent to Daniel on earlier occasions. This was also the same manner in which Daniel was awakened before by Gabriel (8:18). However, it could have been any other angel. The fact that Daniel was still "trembling" when he stood up and told to "not be afraid" (verse 12) may suggest that this angel was not Gabriel, but a different angel who was unfamiliar to Daniel. Apparently, the identity of the angel is irrelevant.

For a second time, Daniel was told that he was "highly esteemed" or "greatly beloved" (KJV) by God (9:23). What a wonderful standing to have in heaven. Of course God loves everyone; however, some people, like David (1 Samuel 13:14) and the Apostle John (John 13:23) for example, have a special relationship with God and are thus blessed with extraordinary divine love.

10:12 – 13: The spiritual realm is temporarily exposed to us in these verses. We are told that Daniel's prayers were heard from the very "first day" he spoke them; however, spiritual warfare between Satan's demons and the angelic messenger delayed his coming. This reveals the existence of an unseen world – a spiritual realm where the conflict between the forces of good and evil, light and darkness, wage continuously around us. The angel told Daniel that he was detained for "twenty-one days," which equals the time of Daniel's mourning and fasting (verse 2).

The "prince of the Persian kingdom" could not be a human king for two reasons: First, no earthly king could physically detain one of God's angels; and secondly, the mention of Michael places the conflict clearly into the spiritual realm. The prince, in fact, was one of Satan's high ranking demons responsible for the pagan affairs of the Persian Empire. The fact that this demon was more powerful than the angelic messenger is absolutely stunning. This is exactly why the Apostle Paul wrote to believers at Ephesus: "Put on the full armor of God so that you can take your stand against the devil's schemes. For our struggle is not against flesh and blood, but against the rulers, against the authorities, against the powers of this dark world and against the spiritual forces of evil in the heavenly realms" (Ephesians 6:11 – 12). The demon's purpose was to prevent Daniel from receiving God's revelation from the angel, and he was so powerful that Michael, "one of the chief princes," had to come and assist the messenger. Michael is called the "archangel" (Jude 9), thus the phrase "one of the chief princes" reinforces our belief that there are a number of archangels. Michael, as I stated earlier, seems to be the chief commander of God's heavenly army (Revelation 12:7), and it was only with his assistance here, that the way was opened for the angel to go to Daniel. Michael seems to be one of, if not God's most powerful angel. He is mentioned three times in the Old Testament – all by Daniel, and twice in the New Testament (referenced herein). Additionally, if we believe Gabriel to be of the order archangel, along with Michael, then I believe it would have been highly unlikely that this demon, as mighty as he was, would have been powerful enough to detain him. This would suggest that the announcing angel was of a lower order, and might explain the reason his name was not given – mere human conjecture.

This scene should alert all believers that we are surrounded by a great spiritual conflict. The Apostle Paul reiterates: "For though we live in the world, we do not wage war as the world does. The weapons we fight with are not the weapons of the world. On the contrary, they have divine power to demolish strongholds. We demolish arguments and every pretension that sets itself up against the knowledge of God, and we take captive every thought to make it obedient to Christ" (2 Corinthians 10:3 – 5). We are engaged in non-stop spiritual warfare; consequently, every one of us as believers should recognize how much we need the power of the Holy Spirit and the presence of Christ in our lives that we may enjoy His supernatural protection.

10:14: This is a key verse aiding in our understanding of the reminder of the Book of Daniel. There are three elements in this last vision:

1) The vision concerns "your people." "Your people" means Israel; thus the prophecy concerns the nation of Israel.
2) The vision will be accomplished "in the future" or "latter days" (KJV). This puts the final fulfillment in the period of the Seventieth Seven, which is the end-time seven-year Tribulation Period; and the "latter days" means at the end of that period.
3) The vision concerns "a time yet to come" or "for many days" (KJV). This refers to the fact that a long period of time is included in its fulfillment and before the vision is finally accomplished.

10:15 – 16: The appearance of this angel had an overwhelming effect, physically, on Daniel for our text says that he faced "down to the ground" and became "speechless." Some scholars explain this reaction by Daniel as a result of the appearance again by the post-incarnate Christ. I reject that notion; because, like with John and the Revelation, once the vision of the glorified Christ had left, the remainder of the vision was accomplished through the work and ministry of His angels. I feel strongly that the two visions, this last vision of Daniel and John's vision in the Revelation, are uniquely related in God's plan for mankind.

The angel "touched [Daniel's] lip" so he could open his mouth and "speak." Likely Daniel felt unworthy to stand in the presence of this angel and to have seen with his eyes the glory of the Lord

Almighty. This reaction and sentiment is similar to that demonstrated by the Prophet Isaiah in his vision of the Lord (Isaiah 6:1 – 7). In both accounts, the angel's touch opened the mouth of God's servant.

10:17 – 18: For the third time, Daniel was touched and strengthened by the angel (verses 10 and 16). The first touch enabled Daniel to stand up, the second enabled him to speak, and the third touch gave him "strength" to converse and prepared his mind to receive the angel's message.

10:19: For a third time as well, Daniel was told that he was "highly esteemed" – "greatly beloved." The angel followed with "Peace! Be strong now; be strong." These words spoken by the angelic messenger were intended to strengthen Daniel and build up his confidence for the revelation to come. The message was most significant and Daniel needed to be at his utmost, mentally and physically.

10:20 – 21: The angel told Daniel that he had to "return to fight" in the spiritual war that is on-going in Persia at the time. Just as Persia was under spiritual conflict, so also was Greece; and once the prince of Persia was subdued, then the warfare would shift to the "prince of Greece." The succession of world powers followed that of Daniel's earlier vision (8:20 – 22).

"Michael, your prince" refers to the archangel Michael as protector of the people of the nation of Israel. Those Jews that chose to remain in Persia after the decree of Cyrus (mentioned earlier) still lived and subsisted in a society of pagan culture and oppressed authoritative rule, inspired and promoted by Satan. Therefore, it was the duty of this archangel to supernaturally protect the surviving remnant of God's chosen people. His duty continues today and is expanded to include the church – we are also God's children, and Michael is our "prince" as well.

"Written in the Book of Truth" is an obvious reference to God's written Word – the Scriptures. Second to our faith, our strongest and most powerful weapon against Satan and his evil schemes is "the sword of the Spirit, which is the Word of God" (Ephesians 6:17). This is why my primary ministry has always been promoting the daily reading of God's Word, and why I include a Bible reading calendar in my books. I will expand on this in a "Personal Experience" following our discussion questions at the end of this chapter.

Review Questions

1) Why did Daniel mourn and eat no choice food for three weeks? _____

   _____.

2) Where was Daniel when he received the vision? _____

   _____.

3) Who was the man dressed in linen with the gold belt around his waist in Daniel's vision? _____

   _____.

4) The vision caused Daniel to fall into a deep sleep. How and by who was he awakened? _____

   _____.

5) The angelic messenger said that he was detained by the prince of Persia. Who was this? _____

   _____.

6) Who came to the angel's assistance, and what is his primary duty? _____

   _____.

7) What, next to our faith, is our most powerful weapon against Satan and his evil schemes?

   _____.

Up For Discussion

"But the prince of the kingdom of Persia withstood me one and twenty days."
(Daniel 10:13 KJV)

In this chapter, we are given a rare glimpse into the unseen spiritual realm and the on-going conflict between the forces of good and evil. In the following pages, I recount, as a personal experience, incidences where both my daughter and I have encountered the physical presence of demons. Each time the demons failed in their assault, and I am firmly convinced it was because they came up against our guardian angels.

Have you ever experienced the physical presence (or even attack) of a demon? Have you ever sensed the supernatural presence and/or assistance of an unseen force – a guardian angel? Does it give you a sense of comfort, hope, or security? Share with the class any experience that you have had that you feel may have involved a supernatural presence or intervention.

Personal Experience: Ronald A. Clower

Spiritual Warfare

Many people discount the belief in angels, demons, and the existence of a spiritual realm unseen to them and the on-going conflict between the forces of good and evil in the world. These are, for the most part, nonbelievers – atheists who do not believe in God and are skeptical about anything they cannot physically see or put their hands on. But, they could also be believers – young, naïve, and non-practicing in their faith and, thus also skeptical from their lack of understanding and/or experience. The one thing each group has in common is that they pose no threat to Satan and his evil schemes. As long as they remain in their present condition, they are earthly pawns [souls] to be fought over unbeknownst to them. It is only when the true believer in the Lord Jesus Christ begins to use his or her God-given talents to the glory and building of God's kingdom that they begin to pose a threat to Satan and gets his attention.

Back in 2010, when I was doing the final preparation for the publishing of my first book, *Jesus Christ, The Centerpiece of God's Universe*, I got Satan's attention in a big way. This book, 10-years in the making, is a concise verse by verse commentary and Bible study on the Book of Revelation, and of course, the last part of that book explains in detail Satan's ultimate fate and judgment from the eternal God – our Lord Jesus Christ. Satan simply did not want my book published. Not only did he put stumbling blocks in our path throughout the publishing process, but he also sent his demons to attack me personally. Yes, you read correctly, I was attacked, not once but twice; and even my daughter was targeted.

The first attack came while I was spending the night alone at our former mountain cabin in Tennessee. I awoke in the middle of the night to see a horrific demon come through my bedroom door and to the side of the bed; he then grabbed my hair and physically jerked my head up from the pillow. As soon as I arose in my bed the attack was over. This very same thing happened again to me one night while sleeping in a room alone at my in-laws home in Knoxville. Though extremely terrifying at the time, both incidences ended as I arose and sat up in bed. I would also add that this has never happened to me at my home in Georgia. A similar instance happened with my daughter one night while she was attending college at the University of Georgia and living alone in her one bedroom apartment. She awoke in the middle of the night to see a large silhouette of a man fighting to enter her bedroom doorway. The demon never came through and soon was gone. Again, the year was 2010.

"For he will command his angels concerning you to guard you in all your ways" (Psalm 91:11).

"See that you do not look down on one of these little ones. For I tell you that their angels in heaven always see the face of my Father in heaven," (the words of Jesus – Matthew 18:10).

"Are not all angels ministering spirits sent to serve those who will inherit salvation" (Hebrews 1:14).

My friends, who are the "little ones" that Jesus spoke of and "those who will inherit salvation" according to the writer of Hebrews? It is every believer who puts their faith and trust in Jesus Christ as Lord and Savior over their life. God knows His children, even while they are in their mother's womb. God assigns each child a guardian angel to look after and guard them against the forces of evil until that person's divine purpose is fulfilled on earth and is called home to be with the Lord. I believe that with all my heart.

I was physically attacked twice, and each time my guardian angel intervened to prevent any harm from befalling me. My daughter's guardian angel protected her that terrifying night as well. Why did the demon not enter into my daughter's room or my home in Georgia? Simple – the Word of God; Satan and his demons fear it! In my two instances, my Bible was in another room of the house, thus the demon gained entry to my bedroom. In my daughter's case and in the case of my home, a Bible is kept on the nightstand beside our beds. Matter-of-fact, I keep a Bible in every room of my house, making my home "holy ground." The Word of God is even routed into a wooden sign at the entrance to our driveway: "As for this house, we will serve the Lord."

My friends, I cannot stress enough the power of the Word of God over the forces of evil in the world. That is why the Apostle Paul wrote: "Put on the full armor of God so that you can take your stand against the devil's schemes … take up the shield of faith, with which you can extinguish all the flaming arrows of the evil one. Take the helmet of salvation and the sword of the Spirit, which is the word of God" (Ephesians 6:11, 16 – 17). Display the Word in your yard, on your walls, in every room of your house and make your home "holy ground" that every demon will fear to come near. Read God's Word each day, give Him praise in your prayers, and thank Him for that special guardian angel that watches over you and protects your household.

My daughter has since, on a number of occasions, seen the presence of a silhouetted figure in her bedroom doorway at night. However, each time the presence has not been intrusive or frightening to her. I have no doubt that this is her angel standing guard. I have never had another incident like the two mentioned, but I never go to sleep at night without God's Word close by.

I'll close with this final thought: I used to have a cat named Tiger who, before he passed away, would lie across my legs as I relaxed on the couch watching TV. Oftentimes, I would watch as Tiger's gaze would become fixed above me as if he was looking at someone standing over me. I believe Tiger had a special sense that allowed him to see into that realm which we cannot. I have had many cats throughout my lifetime, but only Tiger demonstrated an apparent ability to see into that spiritual realm and my guardian angel; and at those times, Tiger seemed very much at ease and at peace.

Chapter 11

Chapters 10 – 12 together make up Daniel's last recorded vision, thus chapter 11 is a continuation of the previous chapter. This chapter is important because it gives additional details concerning visions from previous chapters; such as, details of the Seventy Sevens of chapter 9 concerning the nation of Israel. In addition, there are added details concerning the last three Gentile kingdoms represented by the enormous multi-metallic statue of chapter 2 and in the carnivorous beasts of chapter 7. The prophecy concerns Daniel's people, the nation of Israel, and the impact that the kingdoms of Persia and Greece would have on them. The information contained in the vision was so important that the angel was hindered from coming to Daniel to answer his prayer.

Of added significance, this chapter fills in prophetically some of the gaps between the Old and New Testaments – the Intertestament Period. This was a time of extreme persecution for the Jewish people as they were caught in the middle and suffered brutally at the hands of two warring nations, Syria and Egypt. It was during this time that Antiochus Epiphanes rose as king of the Seleucid Empire of Syria to become Palestine's cruelest ruler, and as we discussed earlier, represented a type or foreshadow of the future end-time Antichrist.

There is also an amazing division in this chapter where history ends and future prophecy begins. Of course, all of this vision was prophecy at the time it was written by Daniel; however, part of it has been fulfilled. The prophecy is a bit complex and extensive for the average biblical student; however, if you like a deep study of detailed prophecy, then you will enjoy this remarkable chapter of God's Word.

Daniel's Vision Continues

The vision with its prophecies shows us the transition of world powers from the Empire of Persia in the east to the Empire of Greece from the west. Let's keep in mind that the prophecy concerns Daniel's people, the nation of Israel, because they will be caught squarely in the middle of this world conflict. Consequently, the Jewish people would suffer greatly.

11:1: The speaker represented by "I" was the angel from chapter 10. In fact he was continuing in his discourse to Daniel right through our chapter break. The "first year of Darius the Mede" was the same year Daniel was given the message of the Seventy Sevens and the same year he was thrown into the lions' den. Darius wanted so much to save Daniel, but he was obligated by his own decree. Recall that Darius told Daniel (6:16): "May your God, whom you serve continually, rescue you!" Daniel's faith delivered him safely from the lions' den and as a result Darius' conversion to the one true God was made complete. The angel told Daniel that at that time he took his stand to "support and protect" Darius; the KJV uses the phrase "confirm and strengthen." This is a reference to strengthening Darius in his faith. This would suggest that though these Gentile kingdoms were under demonic control, their human rulers could be redeemed and used for God's higher purpose.

11:2: Beginning here through verse 34 is one of the most amazing examples of predictive history, much of which has already literally been fulfilled. This section represents the basis on which liberal critics today claim a later date for the writing of the Book of Daniel. These narrow-minded people argue that long-range predictive prophecy is impossible; and therefore, the book is a forgery written during the Maccabean Period after its fulfillment had taken place. But, to the conservative student of Scripture, it represents yet another remarkable miracle in our journey through the study of the Word of God.

Though Daniel would not live to see its fulfillment, the angel gave the message to Daniel to record so as to give comfort and encouragement to God's people who would live during those fearful days. The revelation would also serve as a testimony to all generations of God's omniscience – knowing the end from the beginning and all things in-between.

"Three more kings" would follow Cyrus: Cyrus' son, Cambyses II (530 – 522 B.C.); Pseudo-Smerdis or Gaumata (522 B.C.); and Darius I (522 – 486 B.C.).

"And then a fourth" king would follow, refers to Xerxes (486 – 465 B.C.) who invaded Greece in 480 B.C. He was surprisingly defeated by an alliance of Greek city-states and never again made a bid for world dominion. As the angel stated, Xerxes was the richest king of them all because of his prior conquests and severe taxation. He is also believed to be the Xerxes, Ahasuerus (KJV), of the Book of Esther.

11:3: This "mighty king" is Alexander the Great. He launched his attack against the Persians in 334 B.C. and within three years conquered most of the territories throughout Asia Minor to Egypt; and by 324 B.C., further territories east to the borders of India. Alexander acquired Palestine in 332 B.C.; and though he permitted the Jews to observe their laws and even granted them tax exemptions during certain Jewish holidays, Alexander was committed to unifying the world through Greek culture. This policy came to be known as Hellenization and had a dramatic impact on the Jews.

The Hellenistic Period
330 – 166 B.C.

11:4: Alexander the Great was a world ruler and great military strategist; however, his empire fell and was "parceled out ... and given to others" after his untimely death at the age of thirty-three (323 B.C.) without Alexander naming a successor.

The "four winds of heaven" refers to the four directions from which the wind blows. The following four generals divided Alexander's empire – each knew that one man alone was not powerful enough to control the entire empire:

1) West – Macedonia and Greece – Cassander
2) North – Thrace and Asia Minor – Lysimachus
3) East – Syria and the eastern part of the empire – Seleucus I
4) South – Palestine, Egypt, and North Africa – Ptolemy I

The Kings of the South and the North

11:5: Out of the four above mentioned divisions into which Alexander's empire was divided, two opposing dynasties emerged – the Ptolemaic and the Seleucid Empires. Using Palestine as our biblical center of the earth, the "king of the south" thus refers to the king of Egypt and North Africa, Ptolemy I Soter (323 – 285 B.C.). "One of his commanders" refers to Seleucus I Nicator (311 – 280 B.C.). His kingdom, initially comprising of Syria to Babylonia, grew to include territories as far east as the borders of India and west into Asia Minor.

11:6: "After some years" brings us to about 252 B.C. In an effort to form an alliance between the two empires and put an end to the Second Syrian War, the king of the south Ptolemy II Philadelphus (285 – 246 B.C.) of Egypt gave his "daughter" Berenice in marriage to the king of the north Antiochus II Theos (261 – 246 B.C.) of Syria. Antiochus divorced his wife at the time, Laodice, and exiled her to Ephesus in order to seal the treaty and receive an enormous financial settlement. Shortly afterwards in 246 B.C. Ptolemy II Philadelphus died.

"She will not retain her power, and he and his power will not last ..." illustrates the web of deceit and intrigue going on within these two factions. Shortly after the death of Ptolemy II, Antiochus left Berenice and her son with the intention of returning to his former wife, Laodice. She however, had other plans for regaining her title as queen and conspired to poison Antiochus and had Berenice and her infant son murdered. Once all this was accomplished, she proclaimed her own son Seleucus II Callinicus (246 – 226 B.C.) king and placed him on the throne. This feud began the Third Syrian War.

11:7: "One of her [Berenice] family line will arise ... and be victorious." In response to Berenice's murder, Ptolemy III Euergetes (246 – 221 B.C.), her brother and ruler of Egypt, invaded the Seleucid Empire. He marched victoriously into Syria conquering "the king of the north" Seleucus II and territories as far east as Babylon, while his Egyptian fleet swept the coast of Asia Minor and seized the "fortress" called Seleucia Pieria which was the port of Antioch. By this time, the Ptolemaic Empire had reached the heights of its power.

11:8 – 9: "He will also seize their gods ... and their valuable articles of silver and gold." This is a reference to the great amount of booty Ptolemy III Euergetes returned to Egypt with, including the Egyptians gods that the Persians carried off after conquering Egypt three centuries earlier. One historical source puts the plunder at 150 tons of gold, 1,500 tons of silver, and over 2,500 idols.

"He will leave the king of the north alone." After his victory, Ptolemy III no longer engaged actively in war. Seleucus II maintained his throne within the interior of Asia Minor while the Egyptian fleet controlled most of the coasts. Seleucus managed to recover Northern Syria and some eastern territories from Egypt. Unfortunately, in 244 B.C., civil war broke out between Seleucus II and his brother Antiochus Hierax; and in 235 B.C., at the Battle of Ancyra, Seleucus was defeated by Antiochus and forced to surrender territories in Anatolia (Asia Minor).

11:10 – 12: The "son" of Seleucus II Callinicus refers to his successors Seleucus III Ceraunus (226 – 223 B.C.) and Antiochus III the Great (223 – 187 B.C.). After a brief reign of three years, Seleucus III was assassinated by members of his own army in Anatolia. The younger son, Antiochus III, took the throne in 223 B.C. and, in the Fourth Syrian War, attacked Coele-Syria, advancing as far south as Ptolemy's "fortress" at Raphia (near Gaza) in southern Palestine. However, "the king of the south," Ptolemy IV Philopater (221 – 203 B.C.), was well prepared and waiting, and thus gained a great victory for the Egyptians at the Battle of Raphia in 217 B.C. According to the historian Polybius, the Syrian forces under Antiochus suffered heavy losses totaling nearly 10,000 troops and about 300 horses. Ptolemy then secured the northern borders of the kingdom for the remainder of his reign.

11:13 – 15: Ptolemy IV's victory was short-lived, for soon afterwards Antiochus III the Great assembled a large army and attacked Egypt again in 201 B.C. "Many will arise against the king of the south" was likely a reference to the Macedonian king, Philip V. King Philip signed an agreement with Antiochus and, as a result, gained control of Egyptian held territories in the Aegean Sea and Cyrene from Ptolemy V Epiphanes (203 – 181 B.C.).

"The violent men from among your own people" were Jewish rebels who joined Antiochus III in his attack against Ptolemy V's rule in Palestine; but they were unsuccessful. The Ptolemaic commander Scopas crushed the rebellion in 200 B.C. During this time many Jews were slain; in fact, they suffered miserably at the hands of both the kings of the north and of the south. Two years later however, in the Fifth Syrian War at the Battle of Panium (near Caesarea Philippi) in 198 B.C., Antiochus III defeated the forces of Ptolemy V's led by Scopas, captured the "fortified city" at Sidon, and took back control of Coele-Syria and Judea. This marked the end of Ptolemaic rule in Judea.

11:16: The "invader" was Antiochus III the Great and the "Beautiful Land" refers to Israel. This vision concerned the nation of Israel and the Jewish people. This was why the vision was given to Daniel. Control of the land of Palestine had now passed from the Ptolemaic Empire of Egypt to the Seleucid Empire of Syria.

11:17: In response to the Romans' support of Egyptian interest, Antiochus III negotiated a peace treaty with Egypt and gave his daughter Cleopatra I in marriage to Ptolemy V. The marriage took place in 193 B.C. in Raphia. The marriage was Antiochus' attempt to undermine or "overthrow" Egypt; however, Cleopatra sided with her husband, Ptolemy V, over her father. Cleopatra was eventually appointed vizier and upon her husband's death in 180 B.C., ruled on behalf of her young son, Ptolemy VI, making her the first Ptolemaic queen to be sole ruler of Egypt.

11:18 – 19: "He will turn his attention to the coastlands." Antiochus III had now turned his attention to Asia Minor and Greece. He moved by land and by sea to capture the coastal towns belonging to the remnants of Ptolemaic overseas territories and independent Greek cities. By 196 B.C., he had even gained a foothold in Thrace, thus arousing the attention of the Romans. In 191 B.C., the Romans responded with an initial attack and victory that forced Antiochus to withdraw to Asia Minor. Following their success, a Roman "commander" named Lucius Cornelius Scipio Asiaticus invaded Anatolia and decisively defeated him at the Battle of Magnesia in 190 B.C. By the Treaty of Apamea (188 B.C.), the king of the Seleucid Empire was forced to abandon all territories west of the Taurus Mountains to the Romans. Antiochus III the Great then returned to his "own country" where he died while plundering a temple of Bel in the province of Elymais, Persia in 187 B.C.

11:20: "His successor" refers to the second son of Antiochus III the Great, Seleucus IV Philopator (187 – 175 B.C.). His first son, Antiochus, served as a viceroy to his father, but died unexpectedly in 193 B.C., six years before the death of his father.

As a result of an enormous war-debt exacted by the Romans, Seleucus IV was financially compelled to pursue an aggressive policy of taxation. He sent his finance minister, Heliodorus, to Jerusalem to confiscate treasures from the Jewish temple. Upon returning from Jerusalem, Heliodorus led a conspiracy to have Seleucus assassinated, and afterwards, seized the throne for himself. The true heir, Demetrius, son of Seleucus, was being held hostage in Rome. Taking advantage of this, the younger brother of Seleucus, Antiochus IV Epiphanes, managed to overthrow Heliodorus and seized the kingdom for himself. A few years later, Antiochus Epiphanes had the infant son of Seleucus (a second rightful heir and also named Antiochus) murdered in order to firmly secure the throne of the Seleucid Empire.

11:21: This "contemptible" or "vile person" (KJV) refers to the above mentioned Antiochus IV Epiphanes (175 – 164 B.C.), king of Syro-Palestine. His rise to the throne, as explained above and in an earlier vision (8:23), was accomplished through deceit and treachery. He was a deceiver, coming to the throne with a program of peace. The end-time Antichrist will come to power in much the same way. Antiochus was called "vile" because of his blasphemies – he was without a doubt, the cruelest ruler of the Hellenistic Period.

11:22 – 24: The Egyptian armies had been completely "swept away" and the land was firmly in the hands of the Syrian Kingdom. The Hebrew translation of "prince of the covenant" was "confederate prince" which would have been Ptolemy VI Philometor (181 – 146 B.C.) of Egypt. However, it could also have meant the high priest at the time, Onias III, who was deposed and murdered and then replaced by Antiochus IV, through corruption and bribery, with Jason, the Hellenized brother of Onias III. Not long afterwards, Antiochus replaced Jason in like-manner with another Hellenized brother, Menelaus as high priest.

Verse 23 again emphasized the deceptive and treacherous matter in which Antiochus IV rose to power. Once the "richest provinces felt secure," is a reference to Egypt and later Palestine. Antiochus then invaded them and took large amounts of riches which he "distributed ... among his followers," principally his military. He even plundered the treasury of the Jewish temple in Jerusalem.

11:25: The guardians of Ptolemy VI (age 16 at the time) of Egypt demanded the return of Coele-Syria in 170 B.C. In response, Antiochus IV launched an attack against Egypt in the Sixth Syrian War, conquering all but Alexandria and capturing King Ptolemy. So as not to alert the attention of Rome, Antiochus allowed Ptolemy to remain on as a puppet ruler. Alexandria chose a new king, one of Ptolemy's brothers, Ptolemy VIII Euergetes. To avoid a civil war, the brothers agreed to rule Egypt jointly.

11:26: "Those who eat from the kings" table were his trusted counselors and co-regents. They tried to "destroy him," which simply meant they betrayed him. Ptolemy VI ruled along with his sister/queen, Cleopatra II and his younger brother, Ptolemy VIII (also known as Physcon). This arrangement led to continuous intrigue, and in 164 B.C., Ptolemy VI was driven out by his younger brother and fled to Rome to seek support – and got it. Ptolemy was restored and in 163 B.C., the two brothers settled on an alternate agreement leaving Physcon in charge of Cyrenaica.

11:27: "The two kings" here refer to Antiochus IV and Ptolemy VI, living in his custody, following Antiochus' initial victory over Egypt. Each resorted to "lies" – deceit and treachery while sitting around the "same table" working out agreements of truce. This is reminiscent of the conference table of our world leaders today where treaties are forged, but later become meaningless documents in the hands of prideful and greedy men.

11:28: On his way back to Syria, Antiochus IV became enraged to find that Menelaus, his high priest appointment, had been ousted during a riot instigated by the former deposed high priest Jason. He attacked Jerusalem, restored Menelaus as high priest, set up garrisons, and slaughtered many Jews. Antiochus came "against the holy covenant" refers to his plundering the treasury of the Jewish temple with the assistance and support of Menelaus.

11:29 – 30: After learning of the Ptolemy brothers' agreement to rule Egypt jointly (verse 25), Antiochus IV led a second attack on Egypt in 168 B.C., including sending a fleet to capture Cyprus. However, before reaching Alexandria, Antiochus came solidly against the Roman commander Gaius Popilius Laenas and his navy. Popilius delivered a message from the Roman Senate directing Antiochus to withdraw from Egypt and Cyprus or consider himself in a state of war with Rome. As Antiochus discussed the matter with his council, Popilius drew the now famed "line in the sand," which implied that Rome would declare war if the Syrian king stepped past it. Antiochus decided to withdraw, but in a "fury," due to this threat from Rome.

Chronologically, the actions of verse 28 should follow here after Antiochus' withdrawal from Egypt; however, all these events fell within the same general time frame.

"Those who forsake the holy covenant" were apostate or Hellenized Jews – Jews that betrayed their own people by converting to the culture, customs, and religious beliefs of the Greeks.

11:31 – 32: Antiochus IV Epiphanes was determined to strengthen his hold over his empire. Enraged by his imposed retreat from Egypt by the Romans in 168 B.C., Antiochus directly proceeded to unleash his frustration against the "holy covenant" – Israel (verse 28). He broke his truce with the Jews by siding with the Hellenized faction and attacked Jerusalem with intense fury. He "abolished the daily sacrifice" by outlawing all Jewish religious rites and traditions. He then desecrated the temple by setting up the "abomination that causes desolation," which was an image of the Greek god Zeus erected in the Holy Place and required all people to worship the Olympian god. He then sacrificed swine on the Altar of Burned Offerings. These profane actions by Antiochus Epiphanes foreshadow a similar "abomination" that our Lord Jesus Christ predicted would occur at the end of the age (Matthew 24:15).

Antiochus Epiphanes installed an army to enforce his decree. The Jewish resistance was met by the slaughter of countless thousands and the destruction of their city, Jerusalem. A Greek military fortress called the Acta was established in Jerusalem to ensure compliance.

"The people who know their God will firmly resist him." It was during this time that God rose up from the oppressed Jews, the family of Mattathias Maccabees of the high priestly family of Hasmon.

The Hasmonean Period
166 – 63 B.C.

11:33 – 34: "Those who are wise will instruct many" – The Maccabean Revolt: Opposition to Antiochus Epiphanes' oppressive rule was led by Mattathias Maccabee when, in 167 B.C., he rebelled against the Seleucid authorities by refusing to offer sacrifices to their pagan god, destroyed a Greek altar erected in his village, and killed the king's emissary. He and his five sons fled to the mountains of Judea. One year later, after the death of Mattathias in 166 B.C., the Maccabee brothers, under the leadership of Judas Maccabee, led a series of guerrilla warfare attacks, initially targeting Hellenized Jews so as to destroy their pagan altars erected in the local villages and to gain recruits from among traditional Jews. The revolt involved many battles against the Seleucid government and their guerilla tactics proved successful in their eventual victory and the establishment of the Hasmonean kingdom. After their victory in 165 B.C., the Maccabees entered Jerusalem and ritually cleansed the temple. An independent Jewish state was established and traditional Jewish rituals were reinstated. Judas Maccabee died in 160 B.C. and was acclaimed as one of Israel's greatest warriors along with Joshua, Gideon, and David. After his death, his brother Jonathan was installed as high priest. Today, the Jewish festival of Hanukkah celebrates the re-dedication of the temple following the Maccabee's victory over the Seleucids.

If you are further interested in this period of history, I recommend you look into the apocryphal books of *1 and 2 Maccabees*.

11:35: "Some of the wise will stumble" refers to those who understood the Word of God. They – both Jew and Gentile – persisted throughout history knowing their faith would be "refined" and "purified" by times of trouble and persecution.

The "time of the end" moves us forward in prophecy from Antiochus Epiphanes to the end-time Antichrist. Though all Daniel's visions were prophecy at the time he recorded them, some are now history and some are yet to come.

The King Who Exalts Himself

11:36: In our study today, this verse represents the point where history ends and prophecy begins. For the remainder of this chapter and all of chapter 12, the end-time Antichrist (7:8; 9:27) is revealed in alarming detail. As mentioned before, Antiochus IV Epiphanes was merely a "type" of the ruler to come at the time of the end. Antichrist will do, on a much greater scale that which Antiochus Epiphanes, by contrast, did in miniature.

Antichrist is a political leader and a Gentile who will rise out of the fragmented nations of Europe to revise the Roman Empire – the feet of iron and clay (2:41 – 43) – at the time of the end. There will be a religious Antichrist as well, who will rise out of the nation of Israel. He will pretend to be

Christ, but he will be like a wolf in sheep's clothing (Matthew 7:15). Nevertheless, it is the political king that is Daniel's focus in these remaining verses.

Antichrist will arise onto the world stage after the rapture of the church and conquer the troubled hearts of the people through diplomacy, promising peace and prosperity. He will sign a seven-year covenant of peace with the nation of Israel (9:27); however, in the middle of the seven years, "the king" will break his covenant with Israel and will "do as he pleases." The KJV says he will "do according to his will." Our Lord Jesus Christ, in contrast, told the religious leaders of the time, "By myself I can do nothing, I judge only as I hear, and my judgment is just, for I seek not to please myself but him who sent me" (John 5:30).

"He will exalt himself" illustrates his arrogant pride as he rises to global power. This, again, is contrary to our Lord and Savior, as the Apostle Paul teaches: "Your attitude should be the same as that of Christ Jesus: Who, being in very nature God, did not consider equality with God something to be grasped, but made himself nothing, taking the very nature of a servant, being made in human likeness. And being found in appearance as a man, he humbled himself and became obedient to death even death on a cross" (Philippians 2:5 – 8).

He will "magnify himself above every god." The Apostle Paul called Antichrist "the man of lawlessness" and confirmed Daniel's words with his own: "He will oppose and will exalt himself over everything that is called God or is worshiped, so that he sets himself up in God's temple, proclaiming himself to be God" (2 Thessalonians 2:4).

It is blasphemous rebellion against God and all that is godly and righteous that characterizes this final Gentile ruler and his kingdom. The Apostle John wrote: "The beast [Antichrist] was given a mouth to utter proud words and blasphemies and to exercise his authority for forty-two months. He opened his mouth to blaspheme God and to slander his name and his dwelling place and those who live in heaven" (Revelation 13:5 – 6). Antichrist's tyrannical rule and his persecution of God's people will be "successful," but for a short time. In fact our Lord Jesus Christ told His disciples, "If those days had not been cut short, no one would survive, but for the sake of the elect [believers] those days will be shortened" (Matthew 24:22). The "time of wrath" is our clue to the precise time frame of his reign – seven years. This is a reference to the seven-year Tribulation Period described in the Book of Revelation and the final "seven" of Daniel's "Seventy Sevens" of chapter 9.

11:37: "He will show no regard for the gods of his fathers." Despite his ancestry and upbringing, though it might be Protestant, Roman Catholic, or even pagan, Antichrist will care not, but will seek only to glorify, honor, and "exalt himself above them all."

He will also show no regard "for the one desired by women." Some contemporary writers use this phrase to suggest that Antichrist will be a homosexual; however, it only means he will not marry, but will focus and devote all his time and energy on his political rise to power. Other traditional scholars believe the phrase is a reference to the desire of all Jewish women to be the mother of the Messiah. The Messiah – Jesus Christ – becomes the adversary of Antichrist.

He will show no regard for "any god," clearly means that Antichrist will oppose all religion and worship, except worship of himself. In the middle of the seven years, Antichrist will break his covenant with Israel by putting an end to Jewish ritual and worship. He does this by setting up "an abomination that causes desolation," which is a statue of his own image in the temple and then demands universal worship by forcing everyone to take his mark – 666 (Revelation 13). The final three and a half years of the seven-year Tribulation become the most fearful time of persecution for the Jewish people, and Gentile believers (Tribulation Saints) the world has ever known, and is referred to by our Lord Jesus Christ as the "Great Tribulation" (Matthew 24:15 – 26 KJV). It is a dictatorship on steroids!

11:38: Antichrist will honor "a god of fortresses," or as in the KJV, "the god of forces." Fortresses or forces refer to kingdoms; so who has the kingdoms of the world? Our Lord Jesus Christ called Satan "the prince of this world" (John 12:31; 14:30; 16:11). In fact, Satan offered Jesus the kingdoms of this world, and our Lord rejected his offer (Matthew 4:8 – 10). Evidently, Satan had the right to make the offer. Antichrist, on the other hand, will accept Satan's offer and becomes the first true worldwide dictator. The Apostle John wrote, "The dragon [Satan] gave the beast [Antichrist] his power and his throne and great authority. Men worshiped the dragon because he had given authority to the beast, and they also worshiped the beast and asked, 'Who is like the beast? Who can make war against him?'" (Revelation 13:2b; 4). Gold and silver, precious stones and costly gifts are merely the treasures of a worldly king; they too will be short-lived.

11:39: This is Satan's final hour. The third "woe" of the Book of Revelation represents Satan's banishment to earth at the mid-point of the Tribulation Period: "But woe to the earth and the sea, because the devil has gone down to you! He is filled with fury, because he knows that his time is short" (Revelation 12:12). After a fatal wound (Revelation 13:3), Antichrist becomes Satan incarnate – Satan's earthly tool to accomplish his ultimate desire – to be worshiped.

"He will attack the mightiest fortresses." Antichrist and his Satan inspired forces of evil will come against every kingdom on earth. "He [Antichrist] was given power to make war against the saints and to conquer them. And he was given authority over every tribe, people, language and nation" (Revelation 13:7). The saints are those who will oppose Antichrist and become the target of his wrath and vicious persecution. Those who "acknowledge him" are the ten kings who hand over their authority to Antichrist and become subservient to him. These kings are represented in Daniel's earlier visions by the ten toes of the enormous statue (2:41) and the ten horns of the terrifying beast (7:7). Antichrist becomes the final dictator of the world, and he will "distribute the land," that is seized kingdoms, as a reward to those who serve him well.

11:40: "The time of the end" that Daniel has been so focused on through this section refers to the "latter days" (Daniel 2:28; 10:14 KJV) for the nation of Israel. This time, as mentioned earlier, coincides with the "times of the Gentiles" (Luke 21:24), and here, denotes the last three and a half years of the Tribulation Period, just before the return of Christ.

Using Palestine again as our center of the world, "the king of the south" is apparently a ruler of Egypt or of an Egyptian/African alliance, but it is impossible to say for sure. On the other hand, "the king of the north" is more easily identified. He is likely the same one that comes out of the north mentioned by the prophet in Ezekiel 38 and 39 – Russia. Antichrist "will sweep through them like a flood." In his prior vision of the beast with ten horns (chapter 7), that which symbolized the final kingdom of Antichrist, Daniel said, "He [Antichrist] will subdue three kings" (7:24). These verses could possibly be further explanation of that earlier vision and of the terrifying beast which is Antichrist.

11:41: When Antichrist invades the "Beautiful Land," which is Palestine, he will come against Edom, Moab, and Ammon. These are the traditional enemies of Israel, the territories where the sons of Ishmael, the Arabs, are today. Apparently, Antichrist and his forces will be met with great resistance from them, at least for a time.

11:42 – 43: Egypt, from its earliest antiquity, has been a nation associated with worldly wealth. Egypt and the kings of the south – Libya, Ethiopia, and all of Africa will surrender to Antichrist. Antichrist will confiscate the wealth and treasures of all the kingdoms he conquers to eventually gain complete control of the world's monetary markets.

11:44: "Reports from the east" is a reference to the oriental nations of the world with their military forces totaling millions. The bulk of the world's population is in the "east," and there is very little gospel there. The Apostle John made a like reference: "The sixth angel poured out his bowl on the great river Euphrates, and its water was dried up to prepare the way for the kings from the east" (Revelation 16:12). They will gather to oppose Antichrist.

The "north" is a reference to Palestine; but more specifically "Armageddon." This word occurs only once in Scripture (Revelation 16:16) and it means "Mount of Megiddo." It stands on the southwestern edge of the Esdraelon (Greek for Jezreel) Valley. The Valley of Jezreel is a major travel route through the rugged Palestinian hills. It also separates the province of Galilee from the district of Samaria. Here the armies of the world will gather, some in opposition to Antichrist. However, Satan, the true force behind Antichrist, will send out his demonic spiritual forces of evil to deceive all the nations into allying with Antichrist (Revelation 16:14). Armageddon is an expression often used to describe the decisive battle between Antichrist and his God-opposing forces of the earth and our Lord Jesus Christ upon His return to earth.

11:45: Antichrist will set up his military command headquarters "at the beautiful holy mountain" which is Mount Zion – Jerusalem, between "the seas" referring to the Mediterranean and Dead Seas. Despite having all the military might of the united world at his disposal, Antichrist's evil rule will come to an abrupt "end." He is destroyed at the return of our Lord Jesus Christ to earth by His spoken Word (Revelation 19:11 – 21). Amen!

Review Questions

1) Who did the angel take a stand to support and protect, and why? _____
_____.

2) Who was the "mighty king" of verse 3 that attacked and conquered Persia? _____
_____.

3) After his death, Alexander's empire was divided into four smaller kingdoms. What two dynastic empires emerged from these four kingdoms, and how does Daniel define them? _____
_____.

4) Which Syrian king led an attack on Egypt but instead found himself confronted by the Roman army and navy, and what was his response? _____
_____
_____.

5) On his way to Syria, Antiochus Epiphanes took what actions against Daniel's people? _____
_____
_____
_____.

6) What is Hellenization? _____.

7) Who is the final king that Daniel describes as the king who will exalt himself, and how is he defeated? _____
_____
_____.

Up For Discussion

"And now will I shew thee the truth."
(Daniel 11:2 KJV)

Our journey through chapter 11 (verses 2 – 34) has shown an absolutely amazing parallel between Daniel's prophecies and fulfilled secular history. Though I have read through the Book of Daniel many times, completing this exhaustive study has certainly been an eye-opening experience for me. As I have mentioned several times, the fulfillment of these visions in such detail has caused many liberal scholars to challenge the traditional authorship by Daniel in the sixth century B.C. in favor of a later date during the Maccabean Period after their fulfillment.

In addition, we have seen in verses 36 – 45, concerning the end-time Antichrist, how remarkably close Daniel's Old Testament prophecies correspond with the New Testament prophecies of the Apostle John in the Book of Revelation.

We call the Bible the inspired and infallible Word of God. How have these "truths" impacted your view of the Holy Scriptures? Are you more inclined to read and study the Word on a deeper level? Has the study of Daniel strengthened your faith in God's Word and His ultimate plan for mankind?

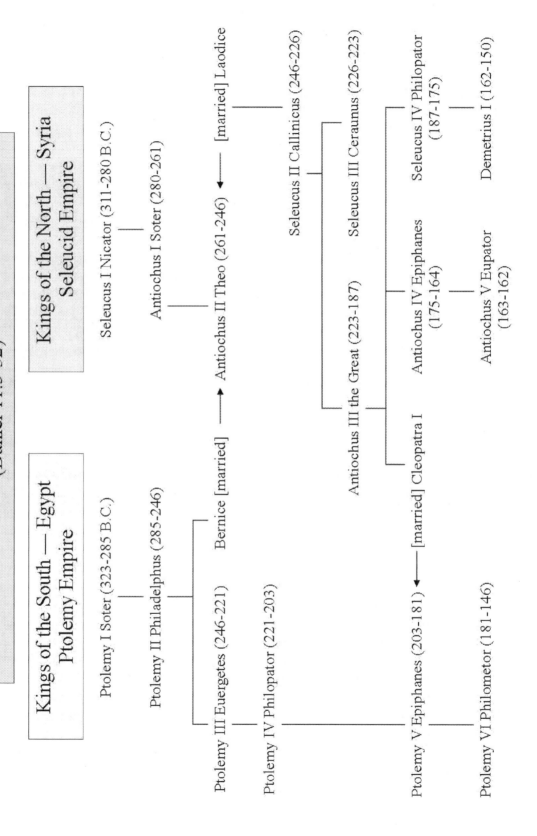

Daniel's Kings of the South and the North
(Daniel 11:5-32)

Kings of the North — Syria
Seleucid Empire

Kings of the South — Egypt
Ptolemy Empire

Seleucus I Nicator (311-280 B.C.)

Antiochus I Soter (280-261)

Antiochus II Theo (261-246) [married] Laodice

Bernice [married]

Seleucus II Callinicus (246-226)

Seleucus III Ceraunus (226-223)

Seleucus IV Philopator (187-175)

Demetrius I (162-150)

Antiochus III the Great (223-187)

Antiochus IV Epiphanes (175-164)

Antiochus V Eupator (163-162)

Ptolemy I Soter (323-285 B.C.)

Ptolemy II Philadelphus (285-246)

Ptolemy III Euergetes (246-221)

Ptolemy IV Philopator (221-203)

Ptolemy V Epiphanes (203-181) [married] Cleopatra I

Ptolemy VI Philometor (181-146)

Another Exile's Latter Days Vision
(Ezekiel 37 – 39)

In chapter 37 of Ezekiel we have the vision of the valley of dry bones which concerns the future restoration of Daniel's people – the nation of Israel. Ezekiel was also among the Jews exiled to Babylon by Nebuchadnezzar in 597 B.C. This vision was given to Ezekiel to reassure the exiles, including Daniel, that God would be faithful to His promises; in other words, to give them hope. Israel's restoration not only had to do with them as a national entity, but also with their spiritual revival which the Lord had promised as well (Ezekiel 36: 24 – 27; Hebrews 8:8 – 10).

The "valley" represents the world where the Jewish people have been scattered. God told Ezekiel to "prophesy," which meant to speak or give out the Word of God. The Word of God is trustworthy; it is faithful and true, and His Word endures forever (Matthew 24:35). Ezekiel, like Daniel, was faithful and obedient to God's call.

The restoration of the nation of Israel occurs in stages as represented by the coming together of these bones that were dead and dry and then coming to life. There are three distinct stages:

1) The scattered bones, as mentioned above, represent Israel's dispersion throughout the world and dead in their relationship to God because of their disobedience and rejection of God's Son, Jesus Christ, the Messiah.
2) The coming together of the bones with tendons, flesh, and skin represent Israel's re-gathering; from their pre-1948 return to their present state as a nation, and even further into the future including the Tribulation Period of the latter years.
3) Breath entered them represents their final conversion as a nation. They are made alive when they choose, at the mid-point of the Tribulation Period, to turn in faith to Jesus Christ as Messiah rather than worship Antichrist and take his mark. The breath could also be viewed symbolically as the Holy Spirit. The restoration of a person (or nation) into a right relationship with God, through His Son Jesus Christ, results in the Holy Spirit indwelling that once spiritually lifeless person [nation].

God has made it very clear: "He who has the Son has life; he who does not have the Son of God does not have life" (1 John 5:12).

The kingdom of David split in two after the reign of Solomon and became the nations of Israel and Judah. The joining together of the two sticks marked "Judah" and "Ephraim" (Israel, the Northern Kingdom, was also called Ephraim after its largest tribe) is another assurance to the Jewish people that all twelve tribes will be represented when the nation of Israel is finally united and restored during the Millennium. The earthly reign of Jesus Christ, the Messiah, over the children of Israel begins with the resurrection of David as their prince (Ezekiel 37:24 – 25) along with the rest of the Old Testament Saints (Daniel 12:1).

Invasion of Israel during the Tribulation

We read above that God has a definite purpose for the nation of Israel in the future, and chapters 38 and 39 focuses on stage two of their restoration and specifically during the Tribulation Period. These chapters tell of an enemy that will come against Israel "in future years," or "the latter years" (KJV). The sleeping giant that will invade Israel, I believe, is Russia.

Gog is the leader of this coalition. Magog (land of) is the territory and is identified with the land north of Israel around and above the Black and Caspian Seas. Magog was one of the sons of Japheth (Genesis 10:2), and his descendants occupied lands from Spain to southern Russia and were later called Scythians. This is from whom the Slavic people were thought to have descended. The Hebrew word for chief is "Rosh," and has been translated "chief of Rosh." This taken as a proper name again identifies "Rosh" with the inhabitants of Scythia. Meshech and Tubal were also sons of Japheth; thus making the coalition in Ezekiel's vision inclusive and led by people descended from Japheth. In addition, Russia was originally called Muscovy which was thought to be derived from Meshech. Other nations will ally with Gog. Persia is Iran, and Cush and Put are nations from North Africa. These are nations with radical Islamic factions and leadership, and are long-time enemies of Israel. Finally, Gomer and Togarmah, "from the far north," will also join the alliance and again represent descendants of Japheth (1 Chronicles 1:6).

God is in absolute control of this invasion. God says He "will put hooks in your jaws and bring you out with your whole army." I believe we are already seeing the beginning of this – the preparation. I do not want to suggest political intent as to why Russia is currently on the move. However, I believe it is obvious to most people who follow world events that Russia invaded and took possession of Crimea, in 2014, primarily because of their need for a warm-water port with access to the world's waterways. It appears as though God has started bringing them out!

The prophet says that these nations, led by Gog, will invade Israel "in future years," or "latter years" (KJV) during a time when the people [Israel] are "gathered from many nations to the mountains of Israel" and living "in safety" (Ezekiel 38:8). Our first clue as to the timing of this assault is the phrase "latter years," which we have already found in our study to be a reference to Daniel's Seventieth Seven – the seven-year Tribulation Period of Revelation. Our second clue is the fact that the Jewish people will have gathered back to Jerusalem and will be living "in safety," that is, in peace. This could only be possible during the first half of the Tribulation Period when the people of Israel are living under the covenant of peace and dominion of Antichrist (Daniel 9:27). During this time the temple will be rebuilt and the Jewish people that have long been scattered throughout the globe will flock back to Israel in mass. The attack will come near the middle of the Tribulation Period when the "gathering" of the Jewish people is complete. Russia and its Islamic allies will come against the nation of Israel "like a storm" (Ezekiel 38:9).

I would suggest the following four reasons why this confederation of nations would invade Israel:

1) The first reason is given to us by the prophet in verses 12 – 13 and that is to "plunder and loot" Israel's wealth.
2) The second reason would be to gain territorial control of the Middle East.
3) The third would be "to wipe Israel off the face of the earth," which is the ultimate desire expressed time and again by the leaders of Iran and their Islamic brethren.

4) The last reason would be to challenge the authority of Antichrist (Daniel 11:40 – 44). Israel will be living under his covenant of peace; therefore, an attack against Israel will be viewed as a direct attack against Antichrist as well.

Antichrist will muster his armies against the invading threat from the North and the South; however, unbeknownst to him, God is orchestrating this entire ordeal. God will deal with Russia.

As war breaks out, God will deliver His covenant people by destroying the invading forces with the use of four judgments:

1) A great earthquake (Ezekiel 38:19 – 20).
2) The troops will turn against one another (Ezekiel 38:21), as did the armies that invaded Judah during the reign of Jehoshaphat (2 Chronicles 20:22 – 23).
3) A judgment of plague and pestilence (Ezekiel 38:22).
4) Torrents of rain, hailstones, and burning sulfur (Ezekiel 38:22). God will even "send fire" upon Magog, the homeland of the invaders as a final consequence (Ezekiel 39:6).

This is God's judgment. After the armies of the Russian and Islamic alliance are supernaturally destroyed, the birds and wild animals will feast on the dead, the weapons will be burned for fuel, and the dead will be buried in the valley (Ezekiel 39:4 – 11). This coincides with the mid-point of the Tribulation Period.

The final three and a half years, referred to by our Lord Jesus Christ as the Great Tribulation (Matthew 24:21 KJV) begins. With the defeat of his enemies, Antichrist becomes the first global ruler of the united world. Empowered by Satan, Antichrist's tyrannical reign begins, and his first action will be to break his covenant of peace with Israel and invade her himself (Daniel 11:41 – 44). He will put an end to the daily sacrifice and erect his idol image in the temple. Antichrist will exalt himself as god and demand that everyone worldwide worship him and take his mark – 666. The whole world under the rule of Antichrist becomes a battleground of war, persecution, fear, and distress. It is no wonder our Lord said, "If those days had not been cut short, no one would survive, but for the sake of the elect those days will be shortened" (Matthew 24:22). The elect are believers, Gentile and Jew. As a result of Antichrist's deceit and persecution, the people of Israel (Daniel's people) reject Antichrist and turn instead to Jesus Christ. Finally, as a united people and as a nation, they will accept the Lord Jesus Christ as their long-awaited Messiah.

You see, during the first half of the Tribulation Period, God will use the covenant of peace signed between Israel and Antichrist along with the reconstruction of the temple as an incentive to gather all the Jewish people from around the world back to Israel once more. Then, as a nation, they will stand and watch as the Almighty God, through a series of judgments, completely destroys the invading hoards descending from opposite directions, leaving them nothing more than smoldering ruins scattered throughout the valley. "I will display my glory among the nations, and all the nations will see the punishment I inflict and the hand I lay upon them" (Ezekiel 39:21). The nations will witness God's deliverance of His people, and Israel will acknowledge God's protective power and sovereign plan for them as a nation. Israel's rebellion against God is "finally broken" (Daniel 12:7) as she rejects the rule of Antichrist and turns wholly as a nation in faith to Jesus Christ – the one true Messiah.

God will fulfill all His promises to Israel, including her restoration: "Therefore, this is what the Sovereign Lord says: I will now bring Jacob back from captivity and will have compassion on all the people of Israel, and I will be zealous for my holy name …" (Ezekiel 39:25 – 29). God's plan for His people will be accomplished with the return of His Son Jesus Christ to earth at the end of the Tribulation Period – Daniel's Seventieth Seven – to abolish all wickedness and establish His eternal kingdom of righteousness. "Then the sovereignty, power and greatness of the kingdoms under the whole heaven will be handed over to the saints, the people of the Most High. His kingdom will be an everlasting kingdom, and all rulers will worship and obey him" (Daniel 7:27).

Chapter 12

This final chapter concludes Daniel's vision that began back in chapter 10. These chapters represent one vision and everything must fit together for a proper understanding of the message. Recall from chapter 10 verse 14 that there are three important elements to this last vision:

1) The vision concerns "your people." "Your people" means Israel; thus the prophecy concerns the nation of Israel.
2) The vision will be accomplished "in the future" or "latter days" (KJV). This puts the final fulfillment in the period of the Seventieth Seven, which is the end-time seven-year Tribulation Period; and the "latter days" means at the end of that period.
3) The vision concerns "a time yet to come" or "for many days" (KJV). This refers to the fact that a long period of time is included in its fulfillment and before the vision is finally accomplished.

It has indeed been a long time since Daniel recorded this vision and whether its conclusion is drawing near, I am not certain; however, the church has to be removed first. The rapture is the next event in God's prophetic plan and no one knows when that will occur.

The Great Tribulation

12:1: "A time of distress such as has not happened from the beginning of nations until then" is a clear reference to the Great Tribulation Period. Our Lord Jesus Christ used this same language in His discourse with the disciples concerning the end of the age and the time of His return: "For then there will be a great distress, unequaled from the beginning of the world until now" (Matthew 24:21). The KJV uses the actual phrase "great tribulation." This "time of distress" is the same period referred to as the "time of wrath" (11:36) and represents a period of judgment upon the world just prior to our Lord's return to earth to establish His eternal kingdom.

"At that time" pinpoints the time frame as the time of the end (11:35; 11:40; 12:4) and the latter days (2:28; 10:15 KJV). Therefore, we can conclude that the end of Daniel's vision here corresponds with the end of the Great Tribulation.

"Michael" is again identified for us as "the great prince who protects your people," that is, Daniel's people – the nation of Israel. He is the one who is going to cast Satan out of heaven (Revelation 12:7 – 9), thus beginning the Great Tribulation – the final three and a half years of the seven-year Tribulation Period. He will protect the nation of Israel during this time as Daniel plainly states and as described by the Apostle John in Revelation 12:13 – 14.

"Everyone whose name is found written in the book – will be delivered." The "book" refers to the book of life belonging to the Lamb (Revelation 13:8). This book contains the names of everyone who has put their faith and trust in Jesus Christ as their Lord and Savior. Here it is a reference to the believing remnant of the nation of Israel who, at this future time, will choose not to worship Antichrist, but instead, will turn in faith to the true Messiah – Jesus Christ. The Apostle Paul wrote: "Israel has experienced a hardening in part until the full number of the Gentiles has come in. And so all Israel will be saved" (Romans 11:25 – 26); again referring to the end of the Tribulation Period. The remnant of the nation of Israel living during the Great Tribulation will be preserved along with their Gentile brethren because of their faith in Jesus Christ.

12:2: "Sleep in the dust of the earth" refers to physical death, where here the phrase "will awake" means to reunite the body and spirit in resurrection. This verse is without a doubt the clearest reference to the resurrection of the dead and the only occurrence of the phrase "everlasting life" to be found in the Old Testament. In this verse, two different resurrections are mentioned:

1) "Some to everlasting life." Remember we are talking about Daniel's people; therefore, this resurrection to everlasting life is a promise to the Old Testament patriarchs and occurs here at the end of the Tribulation Period. These Old Testament Saints are not raised at the rapture with the church because the Scripture clearly says "the dead in Christ will rise first" (1 Thessalonians 4:16). Their resurrection is but another phase of the believer's resurrection and it is promised to these patriarchs because of their "righteousness that comes by faith" (Romans 4:13). They remained faithful and obedient to God. These patriarchs, with David as their prince, will be resurrected and will reign from the earthly Jerusalem alongside Christ (Ezekiel 34:22 – 24; 37:21 – 28).

2) "Others to shame and everlasting contempt." These are the lost of the Old Testament, those who turned their backs on God, time and again, in favor of self-indulgence. They are resurrected for the judgment of the Great White Throne which occurs at the end of the Millennium (Revelation 20:11 – 15).

12:3: "Those who are wise" are those I call Tribulation Saints – that is, all people who put their faith and trust in Jesus Christ as Lord and Savior during the dark days of the Tribulation Period. These servants of God will shine as light and will be His witnesses to the world as they "lead many to righteousness." The prophet says that in God's sight, "all our righteous acts [works] are like filthy rags" (Isaiah 64:6). The only righteousness acceptable to God is the righteousness that comes through faith – faith in His Son Jesus Christ.

12:4: Daniel was told to "close up and seal the words of the scroll until the time of the end." As mentioned before, the "time of the end" is a reference to Daniel's Seventieth Seven which coincides with the seven-year Tribulation Period. We live in the interval immediately preceding this period, and there is still much disagreement amongst sincere Christians as to the interpretation of prophecy. Apparently, all of this will be opened up when we reach this future period. On the other hand,

Christians should remain focused and waiting on one thing – "the blessed hope – the glorious appearing of our great God and Savior, Jesus Christ" (Titus 2:13), when Christ returns to the clouds and raptures all believers up to heaven before the dreadful Tribulation Period begins.

"Many will go here and there to increase knowledge." The "many" are scholars and students of God's Word who "go here and there," meaning back and forth through the pages of Scripture in studying prophecy. Considering the multitude of books written in our contemporary era on subjects pertaining to the end-times, I believe we are seeing more study of prophecy today than ever before. Thus, "increase knowledge" is a reference to the increase of knowledge that pertains to biblical prophecy.

12:5 – 7: These verses bring us back to the vision Daniel had seen at the beginning of chapter 10. We earlier identified "the man clothed in linen" as the Risen Lord – the post-incarnate and glorified Christ. The "two others" that stood on either bank of the Tigris River were angels; different from the one Daniel had seen before. One of the angels asked, "How long will it be before these astonishing things are fulfilled?" Our Lord replied on oath (the OT reason for having two witnesses, and thus the two angels here): "It will be for a time, times, and half a time." This time adds up to three and a half years (7:25) which refers to the last three and a half years of Daniel's Seventieth Seven, just prior to the return of Christ to earth.

"When the power of the holy people has been finally broken" is an extraordinary expression. Power in this context means rebellion – Israel's rebellion against God because of her rejection of Jesus as Messiah. However, during the Tribulation Period, when Antichrist desecrates their temple and proclaims himself as god, the nation of Israel "finally" recognize that they missed their true Messiah; and during those last three and a half years, they will turn back as a nation to God through faith in the Lord Jesus Christ.

12:8 – 9: Daniel was troubled, as in times before (7:28; 8:27), because he "did not understand" his own vision and how all these things would come to pass. He was reminded that these things would not take place "until the time of the end," and thus the vision was to remain "sealed" until then. The sealing of the scroll suggests that the words of the prophecy were complete and should remain unchanged until the time of their fulfillment. In contrast, the Apostle John was told, "Do not seal up the words of the prophecy of this book, because the time is near" (Revelation 22:10).

John lived after the time of Christ's crucifixion, which began the age of grace, the church age. The prophecy given to John was even then in the process of being fulfilled. Subsequently, our New Testament, including John's *Revelation* has given us a clearer understanding of Christ's second coming. This reinforces our belief in the increase in knowledge of God's Word concerning prophecy. A study of the Book of Revelation is helpful in understanding Daniel's prophecies, since chapters 6 – 19 specifically detail Daniel's Seventieth Seven, also known as the Tribulation Period.

12:10: These fundamental principles of God continue from the time of Daniel until the time of the end:

1) "Many will be purified, made spotless and refined." This is a reference to all who have persevered throughout history knowing that their faith would be "refined" and "purified" by times of trouble and persecution (11:35).

2) "The wicked will continue to be wicked." This refers to the sinful condition of the lost; it is permanent and eternal. The Apostle Paul called those lost "the natural man" (KJV) and said, "The man without the Spirit does not accept the things that come from the Spirit of God,

for they are foolishness to him, and he cannot understand them, because they are spiritually discerned" (1 Corinthians 2:14). The Apostle John expressed similarly to Daniel: "Let him who does wrong continue to do wrong; let him who is vile continue to be vile; let him who does right continue to do right; and let him who is holy continue to be holy" (Revelation 22:11).

3) "Those who are wise will understand." They are "wise" because they understand the Word of God (11:35) and are led in their faith by the Spirit. "But when he, the Spirit of truth, comes, he will guide you into all truth" (John16:13).

12:11 – 12: This verse is of utmost importance because our Lord Jesus Christ made reference to it: "So when you see standing in the holy place 'the abomination that causes desolation,' spoken of through the prophet Daniel – let the reader understand" (Matthew 24:15). This is the sign to the surviving remnant of Israel that the final three and a half year period of Daniel's Seventieth Seven, also called the Great Tribulation, has begun. The abomination that causes desolation is an idol – an image of Antichrist erected in the temple in Jerusalem for the purpose of demanding universal worship of Antichrist as god. This image remains in the temple for 1,290 days; that is, thirty days beyond 1,260 marking the end of the Tribulation Period and Christ's return to earth and after Antichrist has been cast into the fiery lake of burning sulfur – hell (Revelation 19:20). The reason for the idol remaining in the temple, as well as, an additional forty-five-day period (verse 12) before the beginning of the Millennial Kingdom is left unexplained. No one has the interpretation because it is "sealed until the time of the end." However, based on the Word of God, we can make some conjectures as to events that may occur during this seventy-five-day period:

1) The Judgment of the Nations (Matthew 25:31 – 46).
2) The first renovation of the heavens and earth (Isaiah 65:17 – 18; 2 Peter 3:10 – 13).
3) The cleansing and rebuilding of the temple (Ezekiel 40 – 42).
4) The resurrection of the Old Testament Saints (Daniel 12:1).
5) The resurrection of the Tribulation Saints (Revelation 20:4).

12:13: Lastly, Daniel was told by the angel that he would die. He would not be witness to these events; however, at the "end of the days" he was promised two glorious blessings:

1) The "end of the days" refers to the end of the Tribulation Period and the beginning of our Lord Jesus Christ's eternal reign on earth. At that time, Daniel was promised to be resurrected along with his fellow Old Testament Saints.
2) In addition, Daniel would receive his "allotted inheritance," which likely means a portion of the Promised Land allocated to his family, thus guaranteeing his entrance into Christ's Millennial Kingdom.

The prophet Daniel's "Seventieth Seven" – the Apostle John's Tribulation Period looms in our imminent future. At the time of the end, this seven-year period will be a time of judgment upon the world such as has not happened since the beginning of nations; and, the last three and a half years, a time of great distress for Daniel's people – Israel. However, this time of wrath will conclude with the return of our Lord Jesus Christ to earth to put a final end to the times of Gentile rule and rebellion against God. Then God will complete His plan for His covenant people. The remnant of the nation of Israel and their Gentile brethren will be preserved and continue into eternity under the eternal righteous reign of our Lord Jesus Christ. Jesus is the Rock "cut out of a mountain, but not by human hands – a rock that broke the iron, the bronze, the clay, the silver, and the gold to pieces" (Daniel 2:45).

Review Questions

1) The phrase "your people" refers to whom? _____.

2) Who will protect the nation of Israel from persecution during the time of distress? _____

_____.

3) The time of distress for the nation of Israel lasts how long, according to our Lord? _____

_____.

4) The final fulfillment of Daniel's vision is completed at the "time of the end" or in the "latter days," that is to say, the latter days of what period of time described by Daniel? Give its New Testament equivalent. _____

_____

_____.

5) What is the abomination that causes desolation, and what is its purpose? _____

_____

_____.

6) What event brings this dreadful time period to its conclusion and Daniel's vision to its final fulfillment? _____

_____.

7) At that time, whose resurrection is promised? _____

_____.

Up For Discussion

"But go thou thy way till the end be."
(Daniel 12:13 KJV)

The prophecies given to Daniel over a lifetime in exile display historically the kingdoms of the world with their oppressive Gentile rulers called the "times of the Gentiles," and their ultimate destruction at the time of the end by Christ when He returns to earth to establish His everlasting kingdom of righteousness. Daniel's experiences also demonstrate how he personally, through his faith in the Most High God, had a transforming effect on bringing the rulers of his time to the knowledge of the one true God in heaven.

I believe God has a distinct purpose for each of His children. Now that you have completed your study of the Book of Daniel, what meaning does the phrase, "As for you, go your way till the end" (Daniel 12:13 NIV) hold for you? Like Daniel, we may not all live to witness the time of the fulfillment of these events; however, has this study given you renewed purpose in your mission as a Christian? Do you feel more compelled or committed to studying the Word of God, or stepping up to lead a Bible study, or simply striving to be a better witness daily to those God places in your path?

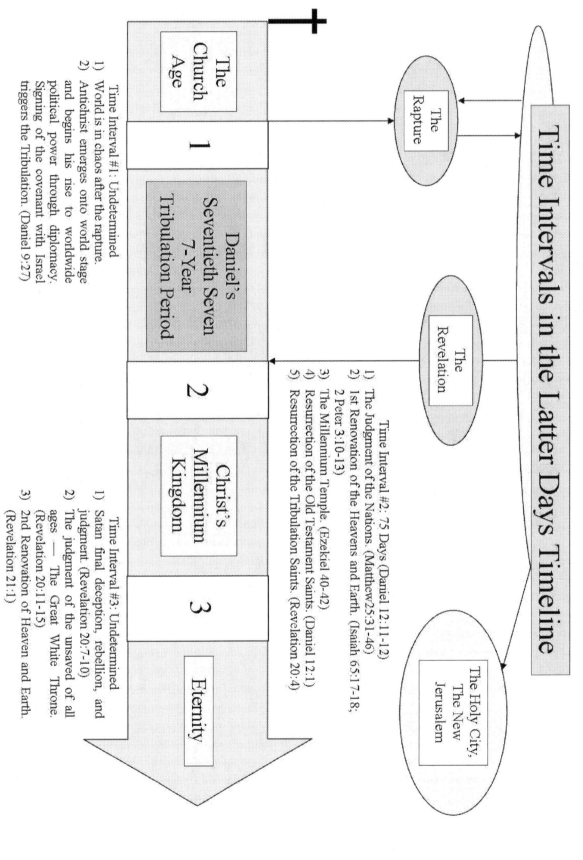

Time Intervals in the Latter Days Timeline

The Church Age

1

Daniel's Seventieth Seven 7-Year Tribulation Period

2

Christ's Millennium Kingdom

3

Eternity

The Rapture

The Revelation

The Holy City, The New Jerusalem

Time Interval #1: Undetermined
1) World is in chaos after the rapture.
2) Antichrist emerges onto world stage and begins his rise to worldwide political power through diplomacy. Signing of the covenant with Israel triggers the Tribulation. (Daniel 9:27)

Time Interval #2: 75 Days (Daniel 12:11-12)
1) The Judgment of the Nations. (Matthew 25:31-46)
2) 1st Renovation of the Heavens and Earth. (Isaiah 65:17-18; 2 Peter 3:10-13)
3) The Millennium Temple. (Ezekiel 40-42)
4) Resurrection of the Old Testament Saints. (Daniel 12:1)
5) Resurrection of the Tribulation Saints. (Revelation 20:4)

Time Interval #3: Undetermined
1) Satan final deception, rebellion, and judgment. (Revelation 20:7-10)
2) The judgment of the unsaved of all ages — The Great White Throne. (Revelation 20:11-15)
3) 2nd Renovation of Heaven and Earth. (Revelation 21:1)

Answers to Chapter Review Questions

Chapter 1
1) Babylon
2) "God is my Judge"
3) Hananiah, Mishael, and Azariah
4) Shadrach, Meshach, and Abednego
5) To honor Babylon's heathen gods.
6) They believed it to be contaminated, unclean, and contrary to dietary regulations governed by the Mosaic Law.
7) He gave them knowledge and understanding of all kinds.

Chapter 2
1) If they could describe the dream, then the interpretation would most likely be true.
2) The gods who do not live among men.
3) To put the wise men, including Daniel and his three friends, to death.
4) In an identical dream given to Daniel by the God of heaven.
5) The four major Gentile kingdoms that will dominate the nation of Israel until Christ returns to earth to establish His earthly kingdom.
6) An unstable and divided form of the revised Roman Empire in the latter days.
7) Promoted Daniel and his three friends to the highest positions in his kingdom.

Chapter 3
1) Pride
2) The worldly nature of a person, or the "flesh."
3) To be thrown into a blazing furnace.
4) Of their position as administrators of Babylon and being officials in the service of the king.
5) They served and obeyed only the living and true God.
6) The Son of God, the pre-incarnate Christ.
7) Their God was superior to his and all other gods.

Chapter 4
1) Hysteria, characterized by excitability and lack of emotional control.
2) The spirit of the holy gods.
3) Angels
4) The Most High is sovereign over the kingdom of men. He gives them to anyone He wishes. He sets over them the lowliest of men.
5) The king and his dominion.
6) The Most High is sovereign over the kingdoms of men.
7) The Most High and the King of heaven.

Chapter 5
1) He was his grandson.
2) King Nabonidus.
3) The Mede armies were laying siege to the kingdom.
4) It was his willful and arrogant pride.
5) He blasphemed God by desecrating the sacred temple vessels and then used them to praise their heathen gods.
6) Numbered. Weighed. Divided.
7) That very night.

Chapter 6
1) Cyrus, King of Persia.
2) False – He delegated his authority amongst 120 satraps and three administrators.
3) The king recognized his exceptional qualities – his proficiency and integrity in his work was unequaled.
4) They had a jealous spirit which caused them to want to destroy Daniel for their own selfish gain.
5) They told the king that all [inferring Daniel as well] the royal officials were in agreement with the proposal.
6) Faithfulness. Faith.
7) Commanded all to revere the God of Daniel – the living God who is all-powerful and whose sovereignty endures forever.

Chapter 7
1) The vicious character and true nature of each kingdom.
2) The Mediterranean Sea.
3) The three kingdoms they conquered – Babylon, Lydia, and Egypt.
4) The four divisions in which the empire fell after his death.
5) The final form of Gentle rule in the end times.
6) The end-time ruler of the world – Antichrist.
7) Christ returns to earth to establish His eternal kingdom.

Chapter 8
1) Daniel envisioned himself in Persia sitting on the banks of the Ulai Canal.
2) The Persian monarch's supremacy over the Medes, beginning with Cyrus the Great, and taking the combined empire to its ultimate heights.
3) Alexander the Great.
4) After the untimely death of Alexander, his empire was divided into four smaller kingdoms.
5) It represents the rise of Antiochus IV Epiphanes out of Syria as king of the Seleucid Empire.
6) Gabriel uses the immediate prophecy of Antiochus Epiphanes to illustrate how he is merely a foreshadowing of the end-time Antichrist coming later.
7) He was puzzled as to why God was merging together the times of the Gentiles with the history of the nation of Israel in His plan for mankind.

Chapter 9
1) Daniel studied the Scriptures, and he learned this specifically from reading the Book of Jeremiah.
2) Studying the Word of God (the Scriptures) followed by prayer.

3) Purposeful praise and worship. Sincere humility and sacrifice. Honest and specific confession. Faith-based petition.
4) Daniel's prayer was based on God's mercy and His righteousness in keeping His promises.
5) Israel's violation of seventy sabbatical years.
6) Because of Israel's rejection of Jesus as the Messiah and the age of grace – the church age.
7) The signing of a "covenant" or treaty between Antichrist and the nation of Israel begins the seven-year Tribulation Period.

Chapter 10
1) This time represented Daniel preparation and observance of Passover and the Feast of Unleavened Bread.
2) Standing on the banks of the Tigris River.
3) The Risen Lord, the glorified Christ, the vision of Christ after His ascension into glory.
4) By a mere touch of the hand of the angelic messenger sent by Christ to explain the vision to Daniel.
5) The prince of Persia is one of Satan's high ranking demons responsible for the pagan affairs of the Persian Empire.
6) The archangel Michael, who serves as protector of the nation of Israel
7) The written Word of God – our Bible.

Chapter 11
1) King Darius of Persia in order to bring about his redemption and use for God's purpose.
2) Alexander the Great – King of Macedonia and Greece.
3) The Seleucid Empire called the king of the North and the Ptolemy Empire called the king of the South.
4) Antiochus IV Epiphanes came against Rome in his second attack on Egypt. He chose not to engage the Roman forces and withdrew his army to Syria.
5) An enraged Antiochus attacked Jerusalem, plundered and desecrated the temple by sacrificing swine and setting up an image of Zeus, demanded universal worship of the Greek god, and slaughtered countless thousands of Jews who resisted.
6) The adoption of Greek culture, customs, and religious beliefs.
7) He is Antichrist, who rises to become dictator of the world during the time of the end. He will be defeated at the return of our Lord Jesus Christ to earth by His spoken Word.

Chapter 12
1) Daniel's people – the nation of Israel.
2) The angel and great prince Michael.
3) Three and a half years.
4) This period is the seventieth seven of Daniel's Seventy Sevens from his vision in chapter 9, and its New Testament reference is the seven-year Tribulation Period described in the Book of Revelation.
5) It is an idol – an image of Antichrist erected in the temple in Jerusalem, whereby Antichrist demands universal worship of himself as god.
6) The return to earth of our Lord Jesus Christ to abolish all wickedness and establish His everlasting kingdom of righteousness.
7) The Old Testament Saints, including Daniel and the Tribulation Saints.

Bibliography

Alexander the Great. 2001.
http://www.historyofmacedonia.org/AncientMacedonia/AlexandertheGreat.html.

Antiochus IV Epiphanes. 2014. http://en.wikipedia.org/wiki/Antiochus_IV_Epiphanes.

Christian Angelic Hierarchy. 2014. http://en.wikipedia.org/wiki/Christian_angelic_hierarchy.

Clower, Ronald A. *Jesus Christ, The Centerpiece of God's Universe*. Bloomington, Indiana: CrossBooks, 2011.

Dowley, Tim, Editor. Millard, Alan, Wright, David, Stanley, Brian, Editorial Consultants. Day, Malcolm, Research. *The Baker Atlas of Christian History*. Grand Rapids, Michigan: Baker Books, 1997.

Huddleston, Warren Watson. *Dreams of God's Love*. Clayton, Georgia: J&M Printing and Publishing, 2002.

Komroff, Manuel, Editor. *The Apocrypha*. United States of America: Barnes and Noble Books, 1992.

LaHaye, Tim. *Prophecy Study Bible*. United States of America: AMG Publishers, 2000.

Larkin, Clarence. *The 70 Weeks Explained*. 2009. http://www.nowtheendbegins.com/pages/rapture/daniels-70th-week-explained.htm.

Lockyer, Herbert, Sr. *Illustrated Dictionary of the Bible*. Nashville, Tennessee: Thomas Nelson Publishers, 1986.

McGee, J. Vernon. *Thru The Bible*. Nashville, Tennessee: Thomas Nelson Publishers, 1983.

O'Reilly, Bill. *Killing Jesus*. New York, New York: Henry Holt and Company, LLC, 2013.

Pfeiffer, Charles F., Vos, Howard F., Rea, John, Editors. *Wycliffe Bible Dictionary*. Peabody, Massachusetts: Hendrickson Publishers, Inc., 2000.

Ptolemaic Dynasty. 2014. http://en.wikipedia.org/wiki/Ptolemaic_dynasty.

Radmacher, Earl, Allen, Ron, House, H. Wayne. *Compact Bible Commentary*. Nashville, Tennessee: Thomas Nelson Publishers, 2004.

Seleucid Empire. 2014. http://en.wikipedia.org/wiki/Seleucid_Empire.

Strong, James, LL.D., S.T.D. *Strong's Expanded Exhaustive Concordance of the Bible*. Nashville, Tennessee: Thomas Nelson Publishers, 2001.

Printed in the United States
By Bookmasters